Head First

Gia Claire

ISBN 978-0-9828911-0-0
Library of Congress Control Number 2011925089

Publisher: Gia Claire Enterprise, Inc.

Website: www.giaclaire.com

Editor: Alicia Caldwell Henderson
ImagiCom Media Services, Inc.

Cover Art: Carole Curley

Front Cover Photograph: Jeff Stella

Printed in the United States of America by
ImagiCom Media Graphics, Inc.
8770 W. Bryn Mawr Ave.
Suite 1300
Chicago, IL 60631
www.imagicommedia.com

Bits of Beauty

Women are the heart and soul of this world. We come in all shapes and sizes, but our hearts are all the same. The love of a woman can do many things. It is only when she understands her power that she unleashes her true potential. Some women take a lifetime to realize their strength, for others it comes easily. Regardless, the beauty of a woman can be seen in all things of life.

When a woman loves a man, he is the luckiest man on earth. Her love can make him do things he never thought possible. Her love believes in him, supports him and cares for him when he is sick. It never tires, it never grows old and it only grows stronger. The love of a woman can withstand the most difficult of challenges. It can overcome any obstacle. It will hold a family together. Her love forgives and overlooks faults. Her love never blames. A woman's love is the presence of God. When it touches the life of a man, he will never be the same. He will be forever changed by the strength of her soul. She will fight for his love…their love…until the bitter end.

Her love is bits of beauty everywhere.

When a woman loves a child, that child feels God's love sent directly from heaven. A woman's love will withstand pain, sleepless nights and temper tantrums. It can heal any wound and soften any blow. A woman's love will sing songs, watch baseball games and play Lego's. The love of a woman can hold a family together against all odds. It makes a house a home. Her love will dry tears and her hugs will comfort.

A woman's love feeds the soul of her child.

When a woman loves her friend, it is permanent and unconditional. She will support and she will give. She will listen endlessly. She will not judge, but she will be honest. She will race to her friend's side in a moment's notice. A woman will carry her friend through sadness and surround her with love when she feels alone. She will laugh and smoke cigarettes with her, and discuss the wrinkles on their faces. She will share everything she owns and seek nothing in return. A woman will see her friend through pain and hold her hand through difficult times. Together they will grow old, having loved each other's children like their own.

But there are times when these bits of beauty need a soft place to rest. Times when a woman's heart is heavy and her body is tired. There are times when her tears are large and her hands are broken. And there are times when a woman's soul cries out to heaven.

It is then, when she is quieted. She feels alone and broken. But God made her resilient, strong and courageous. He gave her a heart the size of the world. He gave her strength to carry all burdens and the faith to move mountains. God made her beautiful and in His likeness.

It is only when she realizes this and understands how she is built, wonderfully made, that she can carry on. She will pick up her chin to heaven, dry her tears and stand tall knowing that nothing can break her. Nothing can drown her soul and nothing can take her joy.

She is and forever will be bits of beauty everywhere.

Dedicated to:

The 100% Club

I accept all of this
as part of my offering.

Table of Contents

Chapter One

I Am Never Out of the Fight...

Head First

I could still hear the gears of the moving truck shifting as the truck pulled away from my tiny little rental home in Chicago. It was the coldest winter ever, or maybe I had just been away for too long. My street intersection was brilliantly lit by the glow of the yellow streetlights. The snow was coming down in flurries not really sticking, but floating. Almost suspended in the cold air, the flurries danced and swirled around.

Exhausted, and exhilarated, I stood amongst a pile of boxes and a crowd of family. It was time to begin again. I hadn't lived here in fifteen years. I had forgotten how beautiful they all were. I had forgotten how much they loved me. I knew I would make it back home one day, I just didn't know how. But my faith carried me through.

The previous two years had all but sent me into a nervous breakdown. *But didn't.* The look in my son's eyes when I told him about the divorce almost killed me. *But didn't.* The stress of commuting out of state weekly to work while going through a difficult divorce almost cost me my job. *But didn't.* It didn't and it never will.

There are things I learned about myself, my family and my friends through adversity. I am never out of the fight. Once you learn that you are not alone, and that you can believe and have faith, you can surrender all of it to a higher power and trust that you will be led. Trust that if you need direction, it will be given. Trust that if you need love it will be shown. Trust that if you need answers, they will be provided.

When you realize that dropping to your knees is not a sign of weakness but a sign of enlightenment, you can persevere. And you can smile again.

I married a man I was deeply in love with, and then after fifteen years of marriage I was not in love anymore. It was not that simple, but the details of how love changes are irrelevant to the fact that I needed to be free. I needed to live a life where people could see *me*... where I could see me.

Slowly, I began to see a new woman emerge. It came naturally and I fall in love with her more and more each day. Now, I am a woman who makes her own decisions. I have confidence in my ability to discover my dreams and follow them.

I feel free to express myself, which means if I want my hair dyed platinum, I'll do it. If I want to wear a sexy little black dress just to walk to the mailbox, I'll do it. If I want to take belly dancing lessons, or get a tattoo or whatever I want...I'll do it.

It's all about exploring my choices and celebrating my freedom to really be me.

In the past I had so many excuses and limiting beliefs. My deepest fear was that I was inadequate, but the reality was I was afraid of the light, and of all the possibilities.

I allowed limited thinking to creep into all areas of my life...but no more. I do what I want, and on my own terms. I give myself permission to let my own light shine. Consider what Marianne Williamson says: "Our deepest fear is not that we are inadequate. Our deepest fear is that we are powerful beyond measure. It is our light, not our darkness that most frightens us. We ask ourselves, 'Who am I to be brilliant, gorgeous, talented, fabulous?' Actually, who are you not to be? You are a child of God. Your playing small does not serve the world. There is nothing enlightened about shrinking so that other people won't feel insecure around you. We are all meant to shine, as children do. We were born to make manifest the glory of God that is within us. It's not just in some of us; it's in everyone. And as we let our own light shine, we unconsciously give other people permission to do the same. As we are liberated from our own fear, our presence automatically liberates others."

So I had to get out. My tiny little rental home was about one hundred years old. Having come from a beautiful 3000 square foot brand new home in a fancy suburb, this should have been a culture shock, yet strangely it felt more like home than any place I had ever lived.

The kitchen had about two feet of counter space, and literally two cabinets for which I was expected to store fifteen years of accumulated shit (well actually, exactly one half of that shit after the divorce). It was ridiculous really, and it made me laugh out loud.

There were two tiny bedrooms and one small bathroom in between. I haven't shared a bathroom with so much as a guest in over ten years, but now my son and I shared a spot for a toothbrush. Ironically, the bathroom was the exact same size and layout as the bathroom I had grown up in. The walls had a bright yellow subway tile, with thick black accents. I had a purple rug on the floor from our previous bathroom, which made the whole thing look just hideous. I had to smile.

My home office was located in the kitchen which meant the newly purchased Crate and Barrel table was used as a large gathering spot for shit I had nowhere else to put. We were so cramped in that little place, but it was our home and it was a place to begin again. It's funny how you think you need a certain type of home. A certain look or style to make it feel like a home and then something like a divorce humbles you and makes you realize that where your heart is and where your love is, your home is there too.

And what better way to complete a home than with a dog. Lovable Dog Max (LDM). I am still unclear to this day why I was in such a hurry to get him. Truthfully, I thought it would be good company for me and my son. I thought having a little dog trot around would make us both smile and create some good times for our newly structured family. A carefully chosen Labradoodle seemed like the perfect breed: midsize, no shedding and good temperament. *Check*. However, LDM was not quite so small. He reached nearly eighty-five pounds and shed like a Collie. LDM was sweet, but he was a crazy dog. So between the size, the hairballs, and his small bursts of insanity, we made quite a threesome.

After two days of nonstop unpacking and countless trips to IKEA and Target, I felt exhausted and a bit suffocated by both the size of my home and the barrage of people coming and going. I decided to head out for a run to clear my mind and get my heart pumping. I didn't really consider myself a runner anymore (but more of a die hard Yogi) though when I did run, it was purely on a treadmill with controlled speed and time.

But that day seemed like a good day to catch some fresh air and take stock of my new neighborhood. As I stepped out into the cold November air, I turned up the music on my iPod to its maximum and began running. The cold air pinched my nose and felt hard in my lungs each time I inhaled deeply.

"The Real Slim Shady," by Eminem, pounded in my ears. With the volume turned all the way up it was impossible to think. I felt my heart jumping through my chest. I felt good. I felt alive. I felt the beat of my feet on the pavement. Although I was out of breath, I felt so alive and invigorated by the scenery and the beating of my heart. I was almost sprinting down the road.

For a moment I felt as if I were running from something, or to something. At the time I wasn't quite sure.

I felt both happy and sad at the same time. Tears welled up in my eyes and began to sting. I wasn't sure what was happening, except that it was good to release my emotions. I stopped in my tracks and bent over to let the tears out and to catch my breath. The salt trickled into my mouth. My heart felt like it was beating out of my chest as the cold November air continued to grip my nose.

I was going to be okay. My life would be whatever I make it to be. I ran from my past and into my future. I had arrived. It was time to get down to the business of my life. It was time to start seeing *myself.*

Chapter Two

One Year Earlier...

Head First

My company sent me to London for a summer to clean up our sales team. It was the best and worst summer of my life. I had agreed to the commute back and forth to London as long as I could be home every few weeks, so I wouldn't be away from my son for too long. My only hesitation to going was that I wouldn't be home to deal with the problems in my marriage. What started out as love 15 years earlier had turned into cohabitation, antagonistic friendship, and broken moments of happiness.

So I embraced my trip across the pond, believing with all my heart that I would find answers, the truth, and most importantly, *me.*

As the black cab pulled away from the hotel for the last time, I reached for the phone to call home. For the past months, tears filled my eyes every time I had to hear the voices of my husband and son. I missed my son, and I wondered if my marriage could survive. *Would this be the day? How do I tell him?*

No answer from the other end.

The streets of London became barely visible through my swollen eyes. I waved goodbye to Covent Garden, to Oxford Street, Leister Square and to all the other magical places that had so awesomely transformed my life.

I pressed my eyes shut to stop the tears, but they continued to drench my cheeks.

I heard the sound of my phone ring from inside my purse. I fumbled to get it, hoping the voice on the other end could somehow make me feel better. Instead I saw a text message that read, "Goodbye Sweet Friend." It was Michael. He had not yet received the note I left at the hotel, but he was feeling sad as well.

A smile crept across my face. The hot, stinging tears began to flow across my lips once again. The salty taste in my mouth was becoming too familiar. If only I could fast forward the inevitable pain soon to come.

The truth was I cried for several reasons. Michael was not one of them. He was my hope for change and my smile at the end of each day, but he was never intended to be more than that. I had no false expectations. He was a dear friend who made me smile. He wanted more, but I just couldn't. It would ruin everything. And who really needs eight minutes of sex to further complicate things? I had enough drama in my life, and the sadness of my marriage was overwhelming. But more importantly, I cried because life as I knew it was over. My life was beginning again and was already taking unpredictable strides.

My flight home was uneventful. I was so exhausted by the time I actually got to the London Gatwick airport that I moved through the lines like a zombie. After being out late for several nights in a row and saying "cheers" to my new friends, I was quite literally exhausted.

It wasn't just my luggage that was packed, but the entourage of emotions, feelings, friendships, and experiences were packed in as well – sealed tightly in a vault that I knew instinctively I would re-open. I was running on empty, invigorated and sad at the same time, truly a montage of emotions.

In my cargo pants, faded T-shirt with the scripted word "love" spread delicately across the top, and my puffy eyes, I knew it was time to go.

I stood over the sink in the lieu, splashed some cold water on my face and stared into my not so sparkly blue eyes. With a half-crooked smile, I said to myself, "Game on girl."

My return flight was only a few weeks after the trans-Atlantic terrorist plot was foiled. "No lipstick, no gel, no lotion, etc., etc.," the announcements repeated over the loudspeakers.

As I watched the other passengers scramble to remove these items from their bags, I stood and stared. Almost mute and fighting tears, I gripped my ticket and waited to be searched at the gate.

The only thing that made me smile was the thought of the sweet sound of my son Joseph's voice. "I can't wait to see you Mommy," he'd said the last time we spoke. I missed him every day. We agreed to wear matching rubber bracelets the entire summer so that we could be reminded of our love for each other.

I stared down at the now faded blue bracelet and smiled through my sadness. The love from Joseph could always lift me up. The thought of being with him made my heart skip a beat. I couldn't wait to see him and get back into our normal routine.

As the plane prepared for take-off, I put on my iPod and stared at the clouds, just as Michael had predicted I would. The blue sky mixed with clouds enveloped me and I wondered if he was somewhere staring at them too. I knew instinctively that I would never see my friend again.

When I could no longer keep my eyes open, I closed them and smiled once again. I would always remember his smile and the way his eyes lit up when he looked at me. That's the great thing about memories. They never leave. They might fade, but you can always bring them back. This experience was one of those that I would relive forever in my memory – for better and for worse.

I pressed my eyes shut and forced the tears back inside. But they pushed their way through anyway. It wasn't long before blackness plagued me for hours.

The plane landed. My stomach turned. It was time for business. I knew what must be done. The question was how to do it? What to say and where to begin?

I was scared and tired and knew this was yet another one of life's pains that could not be avoided. I knew that this moment and the several moments, days and weeks to come would be difficult and painful. I knew the best I could do was find my smile in my son and my faith in God.

As the last of my bags came through the carousel, my heart pounded with excitement at the thought of seeing Joseph. I raced down to the curb as fast as I could and saw the car pull up almost simultaneously. I saw the roundness of Joseph's cheeks through the tinted window of the back seat. When the car stopped, Joseph ripped off his seatbelt and jumped out. He ran toward me with open arms. Our eyes locked. It was as if everything was moving in slow motion.

His tiny lips were pressed into the letter M just like he was saying repeatedly, "MMMMommmmy." That smile was just for me and it was the one that had been looking up at me for the past five years. It always brought me joy and reminded me what love was.

I dropped to my knees and grabbed him as tightly as I could. Our cheeks smashed against each other and we both cried through our enormous smiles.

He pulled back from me for just a moment, looked me straight in the eye. He took his hand to wipe my tears and said, "Everything is back to normal now, Momma's home."

But the next few days passed with me wandering around the house, refusing to fully unpack because it would make my return final. There was going to be no return to London this time, all my luggage was home and it was time to move on. Yet there was something deep inside me acknowledging that life would *never* be the same.

Secretly, I thanked God a million times for that summer. The days and weeks following my return moved at a snail's pace. A cloud followed me everywhere. Even at the park with my son, watching him play, smiling and laughing, the cloud was there tormenting me. Sadness remained in my heart and sorrow dwelled in my eyes.

Finally, when my luggage was unpacked and I eventually returned to work, my heart wouldn't let me go any further. I had learned so much about myself in London. I found peace. I finally found myself, a theory I often balked at when people said they were going to "find themselves." Yet here I was, inside and out, changed forever by this life experience.

I lay awake in bed at night with familiar tears streaming into my pillow. The sadness of my current situation and the inevitable demise of my marriage over the past several years were overwhelming. The air remained thick; my heart continued to drag and my life was not a happy one.

The months leading up to the divorce were filled with fighting, counseling sessions, more fighting and more counseling. But marriage was no longer the reality for us. It was over. And so we decided to make it through the holidays as if nothing were wrong. It was annoying, exhausting and complete bullshit.

Merry Fucking Christmas.

All I Ever Wanted

All I ever wanted
Was your love…your heart;
The safety of your embrace.
I wanted to believe I could be a part of your soul…
that I could crawl into your palm and become a part of you.
Seems so long ago
I could stare at you for hours.
I would beckon your scent to linger on my skin
I would smell your clothes and long to be near you.
And now…
I am left with nothing . . . it's really all you ever gave.
You were great at it.
You took my love, you took all I had to give.
I was great at it and I gave it endlessly.
I look through the photos and I see nothing.
I rewrite the past – the songs we used to listen to sting my ears.
The smell I knew so well is like poison to my heart.
But I am okay.
I am not broken.
This is not my end.
This is not my death.
This is my beginning; through this pain I will be reborn.
I will be restored.
I know that loving you was my choice, and I made it, eyes wide open.

But leaving you is my choice too,
And I choose this day
To stand alone,
To fly free
To breathe again.
I wish you well.
I have no hate.
My choice is peace; find it, go with it,
hold it tight to your heart.
I turn to go, one last tear.
I leap from your palm;
I spread my wings – soaring, not knowing where
I will land or what tomorrow will bring.
Love will restore me.
Peace will be with me.
Joy will surround me.
It's all I ever wanted.

Chapter Three

If Stella Can...

Love

Head First

The days of unpacking 4000 boxes in my tiny home in Chicago were unending. So much of my stuff stayed in boxes because I just couldn't find a place for everything. Truthfully, most of it seemed like crap anyway. Maybe it was the memories, but I think I just collected too much shit over the past fifteen years and I really didn't care where most of it went. So I moved it to the basement and functioned with only the basics, once again, coming to the realization that I didn't really need all the crap I thought I did. *Hmmm, note to self: stop buying so much shit.*

I came upon the box of photographs. One particular set made me laugh out loud. I was about eight months into my separation and I wasn't, for lack of a better term, "getting any" anywhere, with anyone.

I had taken a trip to visit a friend of mine in St. Thomas to just regroup and get some sun. As it turned out, the trip broke my eight-month hiatus and it was absolutely amazing.

Alex was 28 and from New Jersey. He was funny, tall and handsome. We met, we kissed. We ran naked into the ocean, on the beach, in the shower, in the bed, on the chair, anywhere we could. It was amazing. It made me smile again.

So naturally, when he asked me to meet him in New York during my business trip there, it was an immediate, "Uh huh."

As my trip approached, I actually found myself growing a bit nervous. After all, when we were together in St. Thomas I was mildly inebriated and sporting a chocolate tan. And for what I remember at least, I may have omitted a few details and embellished on others. St. Thomas was safe. The possibility of seeing anyone from there again, except my friend seemed slim to none.

The Friday before my trip I volunteered for my son's field trip to the zoo. I froze my ass off in the sixty-something degree weather we had in May with my flip-flops and newly painted "Ruby Slipper" toes.

Joseph had a great time. But I went crazy trying to rope him and his friends together. Most of my day was consumed counting to four. *One, two, three, four kids. OK, got them all. Whew.*

I obsessed about my trip to the airport and felt like I would actually commit a murderous crime if there were any travel glitches.

With a brisk, speed-walking in the park pace, I finally made it to my car. My heart skipped. I plowed my way through the zoo traffic, white knuckling the steering wheel and cursing the young and the elderly who crossed my path. "Move your ass," I yelled. "Pick up that baby stroller and get it the hell outta my way." It was pure madness.

Finally, I arrived at the airport with two hours to spare which was delightful and silly considering how I rushed down the highway like I drove a white Bronco or something.

Strolling in, I heard and walked with just the right bounce to "Don't Stop" by the Brazilian Girls. But the sound of the needle scratching off my record stopped the music in my head.

"I'm sorry, your flight to LaGuardia has been cancelled due to weather but we have gone ahead and rebooked your flight for Saturday," she says with a smile.

I had no words. My head was still trying to comprehend this. The earphones to my iPod slipped onto my shoulders and now the music was blaring into the air and simply annoying.

"No," was all I could say. "This is unacceptable. Your job is to get me to New York – NOW, sister!"

My face began to turn into that of a cartoon character with the color red rising from the bottom of my face to the small tufts of smoke shooting out of my ears. In my head I heard sirens going off saying "red alert, red alert, she's gonna blow."

In typical fashion, she proceeded to get the manager and then all I heard was the tap, tap, tap of the computer keyboard. *What the hell are they always typing? How could so much free text be required to check on a flight? Why do they ALWAYS do that?*

After what seemed like thirty minutes she looked up at me and smiled. "Well, Ma'am, I can get you out of here at 3:00 p.m. and transfer in Cincinnati, which will get you into Newark around 6:40 p.m." *Okay, okay, now we're talking.*

My blood pressure dropped. "Thank you. That will be fine." And again more tap, tap, tap. I was off on my journey.

After another delay in Cincinnati I finally boarded the plane. Zoning out, I felt a little more than exhausted. Having been corralling a heard of seven year olds all morning and all the emotional chow-chow of having my flight changed, I leaned back and closed my eyes.

I took a power nap for roughly thirteen minutes, ending only because I began to do the inevitable fall forward head snap that kept me from crashing head first into the seat in front of me. This was embarrassing. I tried to play it off like I'm just stretching by subtly moving in a similar fashion but in the other direction. You know, just stretching my neck and all. No one bought this bullshit, I'm sure.

About an hour longer and then my plane landed. I scrimmaged off the plane with everyone else and then on to claim my bag. When it came down the poop shoot of bags in Newark, I actually said out loud, "Yeah, my bag is here, my bag is here."

Still smiling, I plopped myself into the cab and headed for the city. I called Josie.

We were establishing my game plan for the evening. Her husband was out of town and she was manning the ship at home, living vicariously through me at this point. While she played a dice game with her kids, we talked in code about what I should wear, whether or not we should go for a drink first, and blah, blah, blah. I was fifteen years out of practice!

Finally after what seemed like an entire day later, I arrived at the Marriott Marquis in Times Square. I unpacked my bags and took a deep sigh of relief. I began watching the clock and getting into shag mode. I called Josie again.

"So what are you wearing?" she asked curiously.

"Oh I dunno. I packed a million things, at the moment, yoga pants," I replied.

"Make sure you have condoms. Don't expect him to have them."

"Check." I replied.

"Oh, and get some lubricant and a tub of Altoids," she insisted.

"Girl, when did you become the expert on all of this?" I chided her.

"Never mind," she said, "Just do it."

"Yes Ma'am."

I did a mental checklist of all these things and confirmed with my girl that I was all set. I ordered room service since the only meal I had in the past twelve hours consisted of two protein bars. I chose a salad and scarfed it down to ease the growling of my belly. Then I had gas. This was bad. I was nervous, and I had gas. *Shit.*

I called Josie. She laughed her ass off. When she could talk, she advised me to walk around and try to fart. Again, laughing her ass off. No luck. I hung up.

I walked around and did sit ups, but still no relief.
I called Josie back. Forget the gas, I'm nervous.

She insisted I get a double vodka and tonic to ease my stress. I wore my tiny little pink top and red yoga pants by Victoria's Secret with the word PINK spread across my bottom. As I strolled through the lobby to the bar area, PINK ass and all, Josie was on the phone with me and we were laughing as I provided her blow by blow feedback on all the heads that were turning while I sauntered (gas and all) up to the bar.

The bartender told me there were thirty people in line waiting for a drink. I gestured to him in a way that says, "Have you seen my ass in these pants? Are you freaking kidding me?" Immediately he took my order.

Josie was again laughing her ass off. I got dirty, disapproving looks from women at the bar. *Fuck 'em, I gotta get my groove back*. I hung up with Josie.

About thirty minutes later, only half my drink was gone and I was warmly and delightfully buzzed. Alex was supposed to show up any minute. Now my fear was that I was going to be silly and sloppy when he arrived.

I called Josie back. By now her kids were in bed and she was waiting for the updates and I was laughing at meaningless things. She became hysterical at my half-drink buzz. Her plan wasn't for me to get buzzed, but just relaxed. But the good news was the gas was gone and I felt skinny again.

I thanked her again for the profound advice. "Get the double vodka," as if she were orchestrating the entire evening from her bedroom, since I suddenly became unable to think for myself.

The long awaited knock at the door arrived. To look casual and unassuming, I walked to the door with the phone still in hand. I remained cool and funny while talking with Josie.

I was still wearing the PINK yoga pants. They were hot.

"Okay sweetie, I love you too…." Josie and I hung up.

I smiled and looked at Alex from head to toe as he came into the room. He requested to take a shower, but moved right in for the kiss and hug combo. This was nice. We were touching each other and reminiscing about our rendezvous a month earlier. Once again I heard the Brazilian Girls playing in my head. My hands drew across his body as my mind was interrupted by the familiar sound of a record needle scratching. *Was my ass always bigger than his? Were his arms this skinny before? Did his tongue try to gag me like this the last time? Oh shit, I didn't see this backfiring.*

We moved to the bed. I enjoyed myself. Things felt good and started to heat up. I attributed my thoughts to nervousness and to my postprandial buzz. I'm pretty sure he was erect when he arrived at the door but there was no stopping the inevitable early explosion. I was OK with this, I think.
That's why I agreed to this, right?

I reached for my drink and decided it was time for another one after he showered, and then we headed to the bar in the hotel. I plopped myself down at the bar for another vodka tonic. Alex was carded, which made me feel weird. Not old, just weird. The bartender looked at me with not one single question as to whether or not I was twenty-one. *A courtesy look would have been nice, shithead.*

So my sweet friend and I cozied up for a few cocktails and resumed a level of familiarity where we left off, admitting the potential weirdness of reconnecting after St. Thomas. After one drink we were good. It was all good.

We strolled outside to have a smoke (which, because I don't smoke, made me really buzzed). I took a drag of the cigarette. *So glad I work out five days a week and watch my diet so I can rot my lungs out with this disgusting cancer stick.* I exhaled the smoke out like a pro. *I'm not right, but what the hell?*

We were in the elevator groping each other. Now this I liked. We got to the room and the music was back in my head. We got it on, and we rocked it like there was no tomorrow.

Later, I started dancing, swaying and swooping, all the while praying my knee didn't pop out. I also prayed I didn't sway myself right into the coffee table because of the delicious little buzz I'd acquired. I was a bit wobbly on the heels, but he was none the wiser. Actually, I felt I was doing a pretty good job for not having any official lap dance training. I had certainly watched enough "G-String Divas" on HBO as a primer for this very moment.

By 3:00 pm the next day, it was time to open the room-darkening blinds and order room service, I achieved great clarity about this entire situation.

Alex and I chatted about music and movies. It was as if I turned the sound to mute and there he was chatting, about songs on his iPod and Robert De Niro, while shoving french-fries into his mouth like tree limbs into a wood chipper. In between bites, I discreetly peeked over at my watch. If I could get out of there by 4:00, I could get to Bendel's and LUSH before dinner. It was time. It was done.

As we made plans for the evening, I nodded and smiled knowing that I would probably never see Alex again. He was sweet and a good, energetic lover, which was just what I needed. But after almost falling into the toilet several hundred times because the seat was left up, and discovering that he had just moved out of his parents' house six months ago, plus seeing him get carded the night before, I decided it was time to cut bait. We hugged and pecked and he was off to Jersey.

We talked two hours later, but we were both just too tired. We didn't want to ruin a good thing. Game over.

I went shopping and had dinner at my favorite Chinese restaurant, Chin Chin. I got rock star service because I knew the owner. So was it worth it? One plane ticket to NYC: $200. Two nights at the Marriott Marquis in Times Square: FREE (pilfered the points out of marital Marriott Rewards account). Trip to drugstore for miscellaneous mood enhancing materials: $20. Trip to Agent Provocateur: $200.
Achieving mental clarity in one weekend (plus a darling new bikini from Billabong): PRICELESS. Look out Stella…you ain't the only girl who's got her groove back.

Chapter Four

Future Self...

Head First

I employed a life coach after feeling unable to sort through the bullshit of my life on my own. After a few years of sitting on a coach spilling my guts to a psychologist, I decided I needed more action – more ass-kicking. He asked me to perform an exercise that involved going into the future to visit myself twenty years from now. *Wow. I can't believe I'm paying for this.* A little absurd, I wondered why I would want to imagine myself at the age of 60. With everyone saying how short life is, why the hell would I spend time dwelling in the future? But, because I was paying him generously to kick my ass and challenge me, I decided to go along with the program.

Alberto started the exercise by putting me into a deep meditative state. I was no stranger to meditation so this part was easy. I laid on my couch and just relaxed as I listened to the soothing tone of his voice and began to imagine myself as he described – a bright light coming from in between my eyes, which was how I soared out of my home in Chicago to the moon. I traveled back on a different color light to return to earth twenty years from now.

Okay. I was following this, but I found instantly that the thought of fast forwarding my life twenty years actually made me sad and I began to tear up. *How can this be good? How can looking at my old self help me in my current state of life circumstances?*

I continued to follow Alberto's words, soft and steady talking me right off the planet. I pictured myself so far from earth that it looked just like a little ball with smudges of blue and green, encircled by the dust of white clouds. I felt the wind on my face, almost in super hero fashion, soaring back into Chicago so far into the future. It was then, on that cold and snowy Friday morning in February that I met my "Future Self."

So there I was sitting across from Gia. She was me. I was her, and yet I was enraptured by our conversation, like I was meeting this fabulous woman for the first time.

I saw her in an elegant condo in downtown Chicago. I heard the sounds of the city below – fire trucks racing in the streets, police cars, horns beeping – all the usual sounds that make a city hum.

She looked at me with such interest and enthusiasm. She sat very proper in her seat with a white cable knit sweater on. Her hair was a dark brown, spiky messy like mine today. Her eyes were sparkly blue and her skin was beautiful. Her huge smile followed me and her hands were crossed gently across her lap as if to take me in, like she had a secret.

I was going to love the next 20 years, In fact, she had already lived my next 20 years. I asked her what I needed to do to get closer to my dreams. What could I do now to create the life I really want? She looked at me with a simple smile, put her hand on my heart, and said only one simple thing, "Keep writing. Have other people feel what you feel."

I couldn't help but let my eyes wander to her face and her hands to see how time had traveled on my now beautiful skin. I was pleased to see that she had aged well; in fact she was beautiful and vibrant. She looked peaceful. She looked wise.

I'm happy to say she looked sort of edgy, like this lady really had it going on.

I wanted to search her place for pictures of grandchildren, or other children, like the baby girl that still lives in my heart. I wanted to see anything that I could find out about her. But instead, I found my focus remained on her.

She had that look that I give people when I'm really engaged; that sort of on the edge of your seat, lean in, eye contact look. I loved her. I wanted to be her, yet I already was.

Alberto told me she had a gift for me. *Ooooh nice, a gift for me.* When she turned to pick up a box, I noticed it looked like a box the size of a large book, like a bible or hardcover journal. She said nothing as she placed the package in my hands.

Again, I noticed her elegant hands, a perfect French manicure. I opened the box and there was a journal. It was a large hardcover journal that I assumed was to encourage my writing. I cracked the journal open to thumb through the freshly pressed pages and noticed that it was a photo album of my life. Pictures that jumped out at me were of my father, brother and mother. It all flashed so quickly, but I saw their faces. I looked up at her and she just smiled.

"Write what's in your heart," my older counterpart exclaimed. Alberto began calling me. It was time to go. I gave her a small embrace, sort of amazed and impressed by the whole visit. Reaching in, I caught a drift of her fragrance. She was still wearing Coco Mademoiselle, my signature fragrance. *Classy lady.*

I traveled away from earth already wanting to return to Gia to see her again and to ask her more questions. I also wanted to check out that cool condo and maybe peek in the closet.

Alberto took me back to present day, waking me up to the reality of my dusty and cluttered home in Chicago. I smiled at the thought of knowing I will one day be back in that classy place on Michigan Avenue.

So what was the point of the exercise? Well, if I can conceive it in my mind, I can bring it into my world. In other words, if I can see my future as I want it, I can make it my reality.

Surely, this would not be such a happy ending if I had found myself with scraggly hair, wearing those dirty half finger gloves, pushing an empty grocery cart collecting pop cans on Michigan Avenue, or anywhere else for that matter. But hey, it's all good.

Chapter Five

Next... Love

Head First

After a few months of settling in, I navigated my way onto the dating website, Match.com. My girlfriends thought a membership would be such a delightful gift. Quite frankly, I think they worried about me dragging them out of their warm, snug marital beds to nights of debauchery.

After all, "single girl" was my newfound status. Never in a million years would I think this is necessary, but I was expected to report back to them with details.

So I tried it and was up until almost midnight posting pictures, writing about me and about what I want to find in my match. The words came easily…type…type…type….

I pushed to the maximum on available writing space and finished the last section of bullshit about things I like to do. You know, the usual: sushi, dancing, blah, blah, blah. I mean, it's all true but conceptually, I'm turned off by the whole thing. It was like creating a flyer to sell myself.

But what the hell, right? I'd just moved back to the city and my girlfriends surprised me with this little treat, so I politely obliged.

I reviewed my pictures with one last nod of approval for choosing just the right ones. I smiled and laughed at all the right places while reading my profile. "Brilliant," I said out loud to myself. A wave of accomplishment and hidden curiosity swept through me. My pointer finger raised and then tapped the ENTER button. Profile submitted. "Here we go."

Around one o'clock in the morning, immediately after submitting my profile, I scanned through my matches and sent some winks and emails to my selections. I looked through these lucky bachelors who were chosen based on my criteria.

"Holy shit, these dudes are trolls. How could they pop up with having seventy to eighty percent of what I'm looking for by selecting a few criteria?" There was just one thing missing. Teeth, or hair, or perhaps they should add a few sections that ask the following questions (all yes or no answers): 1. Do you have pictures of your face instead of your biceps? If so, please provide. 2. Does your interpretation of athletic and toned mean that you only have one set of love handles? 3. Do you have a picture of yourself NOT wearing sunglasses and a hat? If so, please provide. 4. Have you ever been told by anyone other than your mother that you're good looking?

Sorry, not trying to be rude. Lord knows laughing at my-self is my specialty, but it's not a good feeling that this damn computer could not match me up with one single individual that was attractive to me. Not ONE.

So I did some scanning and some scrolling. "OK…getting warmer." A few hotties popped up. They un-doubtedly came with egos and arrogance. Potentially danger-ous, but prejudgment wasn't my thing. So I punched out a few winks and walked away from the computer around two in the morning.

My slumber was interrupted because of the ever annoying 3:00 a.m. bark of my very lovable dog Max (LDM). Appar-ently someone three blocks away was walking their dog and my clairvoyant LDM was picking up on the scent and direction. He felt it necessary to alert me and let me know this was happening.

"What the hell Max?" I pulled my freezing ass out of bed, stumbled down the stairs and let Max out. Now the entire neighborhood knows that he's located another dog. As you can imagine, I gained popularity daily with this barking nonsense. But in the wee hours of the morning, I didn't really have the energy to give a shit. Max stayed out there and ran about, while I waited inside the doorway. He had sufficient time to continue to annoy the neighbors.

Sitting against the stairwell and swirling my Uggs across the steps in a circular motion, the light of my computer caught my attention. *Hey, maybe I got me some takers.*

I strolled over and logged into Match.com. My profile had been rejected, but they didn't exactly tell me why. Instead they listed a million reasons why it may have been bounced back. *Great.* Apparently they weren't huge fans of using profanity in profiles. *Note to self: modify profile and remove profanity in the morning.*

As much as the whole process seemed like bullshit, I couldn't help but notice the wink that came in within the past hour. With a quick glance at the troll who winked, I knew he had no chance of ever meeting me. But I reviewed his profile anyway. I was not fazed by his attempt to impress me through words and pictures of him and his motorcycle. NEXT.

I sat on the edge of my bed for a moment with a wrinkled brow and said quietly, "Chicago is one of the most popular cities in the country to live. There's gotta be some nice men available." I pushed Max's hair out of his eyes as he looked at me sleepily.

After my little bedtime pep talk, I awoke like a child on Christmas morning. I rushed to my computer to see how many exciting people had found this fabulous girl "wink" worthy. The realization that I had just looked at my computer about four hours ago didn't faze me as I stared blankly at the screen.

All I could say was "Huh!" My laughter filled the room. The thought of this whole thing was really entertaining and it distracted me from all the other bullshit going on in my life. Within the first week of being on Match, there were over 500 views on my profile. Now this was becoming a numbers game to me. I delighted in the fact that so many guys had checked me out, even though I lamented that 499 of them weren't dating material.

However, within the first week I managed to find a candidate who was actually date worthy. *Exciting.* We agreed to have drinks in a trendy bar in Lincoln Park on Friday night. This was my first official post-divorce date.

"We should grab a drink." Tim's email said. Scan profile. *Check.* View picture. *Handsome picture. Check.*

"You got it." I emailed back to him. We exchanged numbers and spoke over the phone. He was funny. And I like funny, funny is good. "OK Tim. You got yourself a date." First date. *Check.* Before I dug through my closet for the perfect outfit, I sent Tim a quick email to confirm our time and location.

His reply read, "Oh, was that *this* Friday night?"

"Ummm…what the fuck? What part of FRIDAY don't you understand? Are you kidding me?" I emailed back.

Moments later Tim called and said he got all caught up with work, and *blah, blah, blah.*

"Hi Gia, hey you're not going to believe this, but I lost my phone in the airport." I rolled my eyes. As he droned on and on about his bullshit, I just interrupted him and said, "Yeah, this ain't working Tim."

"Oh man, I'm so sorry about the mix up," he said.

"No problem Tim, it's all good. Maybe some other time." He seemed funny on the phone, very nice actually, but the dude obviously had no clue. That was it. No second chance. I hung up the phone.

"This is great…just frickin' great."

I told my brother and sister-in-law about my cancellation. They must have felt sorry for me because about 20 minutes later, my ten-year-old niece knocked on my door.

"Hey, Sammy. Watcha doin'?" I asked. In her young, honest as can be voice, she said, "Dad told me to come over and keep you company." *Nice, real nice. Now I'm getting the pity visit from my kid niece.*

Around 10:00 p.m., my sister-in-law, AJ and I decided to go out. AJ was like a real sister to me. We were the same age, loved the same things and became great friends in the past year. AJ was a combination of Jennifer Aniston and Jennifer Lopez. She was beautiful inside and out, had all the right curves, and was a helluva lotta fun.

Make no mistake though, AJ and I had some real soul-searching discussions, but we knew how to keep it light, how to support each other and enjoy our friendship. She was my perfect partner in crime that night and many others. *So what the hell? I already had an outfit picked out, why waste it?*

By then, Tim called again with great remorse for screwing up the night.

"Gia, I feel terrible about messing up your night, can I please meet you somewhere for a drink?"

"Well, you did really screw up, I'm not gonna lie to ya, but sure, what the hell?" There was no harm in meeting him and putting the whole story together. And that's exactly what happened.

Tim strolled into Kooba's with his alleged best friend at about 10:30 p.m. He apparently identified me right away, sauntered on up and proudly stuck out his hand for a shake. He caught me in mid laugh with AJ. My mouth was wide open. My expression said it all. *Who the hell are you? And why are you tugging on my sleeve like a two-year-old?*

"Hi Gia, I'm Tim." This is the type of Match date I referred to as the NO LOOK Guy. He looked NOTHING like his picture and the differences usually leaned toward the negative.

"No you're not," I said. He was adamant that he was, so I put my palm up and said, "License. Gimme the license."

Tim handed it over. Sure enough, the State of Illinois picture looked exactly like the one on Match. Unfortunately, neither one of these pictures looked like the man who stood in front of me, who by the way, was half crocked and had a stupid ass grin on his face.

I excused myself and headed to the ladies room. In the restroom, frustrated, I started pacing. *What to do to get out of this one?*

Back at the bar, my sister-in-law grinned while the two dorks chatted her ear off. Tim's friend seemed like a decent guy though. Not bad looking. Maybe I could just swap out Tim and move over to his friend.

But now Tim was attempting to play the piano on my arm while sloshing his words around. I ignored him and ordered a shot of vodka. "Make it two," I told the bartender.

Slam…slam…life was better, but it was about time to get my fly ass outta there.

AJ leaned over to me. "When you were in the ladies room, Tim asked if I thought you'd let him touch your ass." *Classy*. And with that…

"Tim, it's been a pleasure." I shook his hand. He attempted to kiss my hand…with his tongue. I maneuvered out of his reach and took a small bow.

"Au revoir." AJ and I were out. We took our shit down the road to continue what started out as a very lovely evening. NEXT.

That was one of the most uneventful dates I had during this time. My lesson from the experience is that some people are not very honest about themselves, or they have a very different opinion of themselves than the way the rest of the world sees them.

Another example: the Actor. Jackson had some very hot pics on the web site – really tall, strong jaw, full head of hair and just really awesome. But he wasn't very literate, or articulate on the phone. OK, that was my cue to walk, but a little voice inside me told me to ride it out. This is usually where things got interesting.

After a week of texting and talking, we were getting along really well. It's strange how people can say anything about themselves on a text message…and this guy said a lot. By the time we were about to meet, he had all but confessed his love to me. He was always sending me model-esque pictures of himself and telling me how perfect I was for him. *Who would not love that?*

So we met, we kissed…and I stopped him short at the top of the key (translation: did not make it to the basket). I am a sucker for the tall thing, but this guy had no game.

As it turned out, he looked a little like the actor in the pics, except for the ten pound addition around his waist. I didn't expect that. *Another note to self: always get pics that show teeth.* Jackson's were as yellow as a phone book. And then, one date later, Jackson confessed that this was all "too intense" for him and he ran for the hills. *Now, what was that? Too intense? Are you kidding me?* I didn't need this shit. NEXT.

Before I had the chance though, Jeff entered into the scene. His picture was cute. His words were flattering and assertive. I gave him my phone number and really should've known from the first conversation things just weren't going to work out. But when dealing with guys like this, my interest was in playing out the scenario to see where it could go. Really, you can't prejudge people on the phone, everyone is nervous.

Jeff owned a ladies shoe boutique. He had me at "shoe." He must be a cool guy. Fine Italian ladies shoes, are you kidding me? *Nice.*

So we agreed to meet up at his store. Oh by the way, he had no vehicle, a big negative on the pro/con list.

Outside of his store, I watched him through the window. He was a good looking guy, but I felt nothing. There was no chemistry, no skip…no sweat…crap. The truth is, when this happens, my first reaction is to just turn on my heel and leave. Just being honest – not shitty. If men and women wanted to start up a friendship website, then fine. No problem staying for that, who are we kidding? But there was a pair of boots that caught my eye, so what would it hurt to wander around the store and wait for him to finish up? I browsed the store and he barked orders at his customers.

He told them what they wouldn't like and what they would like. A man was on his cell phone and Jeff actually picked up the little sign on his counter that said, "Please, no cell phone use." and shoved it right up to his face to illustrate the point.

My second, third, and fourth reaction was to leave, but if I left could I still buy the boots? Or would that be socially inappropriate? They were beautiful. Italian leather, extremely high and very pointy. They were $450. Not exactly a boot budget that could be justified so soon after my divorce.

"Wow, this store is so amazing!" I exclaimed when Jeff came over to greet me. The assortment of shoes, bags and the few dresses he sold were absolutely beautiful. It really was a cool store and very hip. "You have such a great variety of things here, I could buy them all!" *Not really, I could barely afford the least expensive boots.*

"Great, I'm so glad you like it. There are lots of things I want you to try on." I grinned like a kid in a candy store.
First, Jeff brought out some shoes for me to try on – very Cinderella. He pulled off my boots and looked at the label. Banana Republic. My boots were a beautiful pair of leather snakeskin, which I LOVED, and wore out to almost transparent soles. He scoffed at the label and continued to bring out boots and shoes. I didn't want to seem cheap, but damn, these shoes were expensive. As it turned out, he gave me a beautiful (almost Dior) black suede, just above the knee-length boots with a slight platform elevation. They were

smoking hot. It felt like I should be on my way to a KISS concert, minus the star around my eye.

I also bought the bone colored pointy boots that he politely discounted to 50% off. Me likey this date so far. He seemed a little intense, but it was all good.

I drove him to his place so he could drop his things before dinner. We went to Blue Agave, a very delicious Mexican restaurant. It was here that the red flags popped up like tulips in the spring. He didn't ask ANYTHING about me or my life…it was all about him. He was a DJ…all his stores…blah, blah, blah.

Bored, I ordered the largest item on the menu and ate every last crumb. This should've been a turn off, ya know; a girl who eats too much, but Jeff didn't even notice. How could he? The entire conversation was him talking with himself. Every time I attempted to ask him a question, he'd say, "Well you read my profile right? It's all in the profile," as if my precious time was spent studying his profile. This was not the bar exam. Screw it. I'm out.

I declined (double declined, if that were possible) the offer to go back to his place, especially with all that Mexican food, my tummy was rumbling. But before I could come up with something witty and smart, he somehow got me to agree to a second date the VERY NEXT DAY. Shit! It was the boots. It was a courtesy second date, and it was because of the boots. Date number two took a turn to Crazytown when we stopped briefly at his apartment to "drop his things." He raved about a turkey he'd made over the weekend that I just needed to try it. I politely declined, mint gum and all, but he wouldn't take no for an answer.

In ten seconds flat he pulled out all of the Tupperware and shoved food into my mouth – turkey, stuffing, potatoes. It was actually pretty good and I couldn't turn it away. What happened next is what had to be the key driver to his single-dome.

He took the fork and cleaned it three times with soap and water, dried it, and then put it into the dishwasher. Then he took the dishrag and washed the sink three times and dried it so not even a drop of water was noticeable.

Imagining myself standing on a bus full of crazy people and reaching for the pulley thing so I could get off at the next stop, I stared at him as if I were a germ carrying leper.

We walked in silence as we headed to the restaurant, which turned out to be another night of gastrointestinal bloating. I swear, I just sat there and wondered how someone could have so little to ask another person. Was he actually surprised that he was single? Forget the OCD. He had no interest in anyone else but himself. He talked a lot about his DJ days, at least an hour or so. It was all techno, which I do not care for. He refused to accept that I didn't like it, so what the hell? Why do I talk at all?

I ordered two entrees and shoveled food in like a chip-munk stocking up for the winter. He barely ate, but then again, how could he with all the talking?

As predicted, my tummy was bloated. I really just wanted to go home and sleep. Instead, while he waited for desert, I excused myself and headed to the restroom. So sleepy and bored, I sat on the can fully clothed and called my friend just to say, "Hi."

This was nice. On a date and sitting in the can chatting with a friend. When I returned Jeff had a look of curious concern on his face. By the time the date was over, it was definitely time to make a break for the car. But my new boots would only let me go so fast. They weren't broken in yet and they hurt like a mother. Plus, I didn't really know where I was, so finding the car was a bit challenging. Yet it was a risk I was willing to take to get the hell outta there.

BUT before I could, Jeff insisted I drop in to his place for the CD he made especially for me. *Shit...shit…shit. Why couldn't I have just cut bait? Fucking boots!*

So we got up to his apartment and I stood there as frigid as those long icicles that hang outside a window – unbreakable and frozen (and a little hairy from the snow). He stepped into the other room and returned a minute later with a stack of CDs that was literally two feet high. *What the hell? Did he lose it? Was it like looking for a needle in a haystack?* I wanted to say, "Look dude, I'll just take the first one on the stack and I'm out." The words wouldn't come out. He insisted on playing the music. So there I sat, in my winter coat, bloated, hot and miserable. He acted like he was back at Studio 54 pumping out the tunes like he did in his glory days. He had that DJ dance that was really only from the waste up. "Sounds all the same to me," I said. That really pissed Jeff off. He was convinced that the previous twenty CDs he'd just skimmed through all sound distinctly different. While the music blared and the bass boomed, he ran in from the other room and pulled out all of his ticket stubs from concerts he had attended in the 1980's.

Are you fucking kidding me? I had to sit through ticket stub after ticket stub while this crazy bastard took a trip down memory lane. I mean, did I really care that he saw Motley Crue or Duran Duran?

Finally, after what seemed like FOREVER, I told him I was tired and needed to go. There was no way I could take another minute piled up in my scarf and jacket, listening to this music and sweating my ass off.

But before I could even make it to the door, he insisted AGAIN that I look at a You Tube video of an artist he liked. *Mother F…, this guy is relentless.*

He stood over my shoulder and scanned his computer. He took me to a video of a band called "Unter Noll." I stared at the screen. A young girl was singing something in a language I couldn't even recognize. She was screaming and was clothed in bandages with blood. That was her outfit, blood and bandages. He went on and on about her.

"So…what does Unter Noll stand for?" I asked him.

He smiled and said, "Almost dead."

"ALRIGHTY THEN." Maybe this was how I was going

to die. In some other room he had some very tortuous devices that would render ME "Unter Noll." I stared at the screen and just shook my head. This guy was the Mayor of Crazytown...population one.

When the opportunity presented itself, I busted out of there like my hair was on fire.

"No thanks. I can make it to the car." I rejected his assistance. My feet were hot, sweaty and swollen, which made the boots feel like vices on my toes. But I ran down those city blocks like I was Edwin Moses going for the Gold Medal.

Note to self: never, never, ever go on a courtesy date. It just isn't worth it. All it got me was gas and a little urinary incontinence during my mile long stretch to the car. But damn those boots were SMOKIN'! *It would be wrong to go back for more shoes though, right?*

Chapter Six

Fly Me to the Moon...

Head First

My life was going great, amazing actually – all things considered. I enjoyed being close to my family, and living in Chicago, the greatest city ever.

However, life was still going on around me. Things were still happening to people in my life. My relatives were aging and time was marching on.

My grandmother was 93 years old. And for the past ten years, I missed chances to have lunch with her or take her to movies. It was time to make up for that lost time.

On the weekends I didn't have my son, I picked my grandmother up early on Sundays and spent the day with her. She helped me fold my laundry. She loved helping me. I saved my laundry for two weeks, so naturally it got pretty wrinkled. Grandma complained about it. Yet I saved it for her anyway. There was no winning with her. It was cute.

Grandma was about five feet tall. She had a Dowager's hump and sandy brown hair that was always done up "Grandma style." It was the kind of hairdo that gets done every two weeks, set with rollers. She wore her signature polyester pants and a dressy sweater or sweatshirt that usually read "World's Best Grandma." She always wore perfume and makeup, well at least a little lipstick. It was adorable really. SHE was adorable.

These afternoons were precious to me and for her too, I'm sure. Usually we'd have a nice dinner and catch a movie before the end of our night. We always listened to a play mix on my iTunes titled, respectfully, "Grandma." It held all of her favorite tunes by Dean Martin, Frank Sinatra and Tony Bennett. We always played the music pretty loud because Grandma was deaf in one ear.

It always made me smile to see the sweet look on her face when her songs came on. She'd stare off into space as if she were capturing some memory, some wonderful time, or perhaps a man.

I decided to tell her about Thomas. She was really a great listener. Or perhaps it was that she couldn't really hear, I'm not sure. But she shared a story about a drummer with me. A man she had a brief affair with. As it turned out, Grandma was quite a busy lady in her younger years. We chatted about her husbands. Yes, that was plural. She had some very interesting stories – she lived a good life.

We talked often about men and relationships. I almost fell over laughing one day when Grandma asked what a dildo was. It was hard trying to keep a straight face while describing what a dildo was. *Nice.* We laughed. We had lots of laughs.

One Sunday while listening to "Fly Me to the Moon" by Tony Bennett, a slow and wonderful version of that song, Grandma sat staring out the window. A pile of towels sat upon her lap. She had a deep look of sadness that I felt certain was a memory of a man. It broke my heart. I went up to her and extended my hand.

"May I have this dance?" Grandma snapped out of her trance and smiled up at me. She probably thought I was crazy, but I grabbed her hand anyway and lifted her slowly and carefully out of the chair. Grandma felt at least two feet shorter than me. She stood wobbly at first, but then as our hands met, she seemed to enjoy the moment.

Holding her hand, tiny and bent from arthritis, tightly in my own, we swayed gently from side to side. She seemed to just float down memory lane. The smell of her hairspray and perfume drifted up to my nose. This was a moment to freeze in my own memory. One day I would look back and remember the two of us dancing in the center of my kitchen to this song, with four baskets of laundry just waiting to be folded, and a dog bounding around us barking and playing. It felt good to hold my dear, sweet grandmother in my arms.

The music carried the two of us away from everything. Her heart seemed to yearn for her younger days. My own heart longed its own desires. Regret seemed to poor from her eyes. She longed for something, still. There was something unfinished in her life.

I walked her slowly back to her chair. It was a beautiful moment for me and Gram. Funny how God can turn back time. I had missed this beautiful soul all these years. Here we were back together again and talking about men, listening to music and enjoying meals together. I thought this was our last dance. Grandma's health began to fail after a fall that occurred during a brief hospital stay. She was unable to live in her apartment on her own. I was in denial and continued to save my laundry for weeks. Grandma would be strong enough to help me fold it, she had to be. It took her a few months but the old girl got back on her feet. We had to move her to an assisted living place. She hated it, but she was unstable and needed care that none of us could provide.

Before long, Gram and I resumed our usual schedule of laundry and dancing. It was delightful to share my secrets with Gram once again. We talked about men, and she giggled every time she attempted to fold one of my tiny thongs, or lace panties. She'd hold them up and say, "Whooo hoooo."

Occasionally, with increasing frequency she forgot people and details, but I helped her along. Every minute with her was enjoyable. One Sunday while driving her home after a long day of being together, she looked at me with her beautiful little smile and said, "You know what? That Joey (my brother) has always been my favorite."

"Gram, are you kidding me? You're actually telling me this?"

She said, "Well, I've known him longer and I've had more time with him."

Clearly, dumbfounded and not really caring, just having some fun with her, I looked at her and said, "Gram…you've only known him TWO years longer, are you kidding me?" But she stuck to her guns on this one. "Yep. He's my favorite." Two words about my brother…Javier Perfecto.

Chapter Seven

Head First

I referred to my divorce as the fire. If you think about it, it makes a lot of sense. The only thing left is ash and rubble. Right now, things are black and unrecognizable. The air has a different smell and the sounds of joy and happiness have drifted off with the flames. The only sound remaining is the hiss of the smoldering ashes.

After settling into Chicago, my new position and my new life, it was time to schedule a business trip back to Ohio. It wouldn't take more than a day or two to complete the trip. But the thought was dreadful because of the rush of memories sure to hit me. I braced myself for the ghosts as my car pointed east.

My car rounded the familiar turn onto Bullshit Drive and reminded me of the hundreds of times I'd driven this path in the past five years. Rounding the corner of my son's school bus stop, I caught my breath thinking of his first days of school riding the bus. Joseph walked so bravely to the bus and had turned to give me one last smile and wave before he hopped up the steps. The memory brought tears to my eyes.

Now almost ten years old, Joseph was five foot four and wore a size eleven shoe, always towering a head or two over his peers. His hair is brown and his eyes are the color of milk chocolate.

No doubt my little cherub was on his way to a career similar to LeBron James if he played his cards right.

But that day, on his first day of school, he looked like a sweet little boy on his way to the rest of his life.

It was time to go back to our home and say goodbye to the ghosts…to forgive myself…to forgive my ex-husband. In the cold of winter the neighborhood looked solemn. There was no one out. There would be no, "Hi. How have you been?" conversations, but I was grateful for that.

My car crept up the driveway with the crunch of snow under my tires as if to resist my presence there. I parked, walked up to the garage door and dialed the code to enter. In no time at all, I was in the garage with the door shut quickly behind me.

"Why should I feel sad?" I asked myself. "I am in such a better place now. The divorce is what I wanted. Why the hell did I even come back here? Just so I could torture myself? Shit, I'm stupid."

Walking in through the garage, the feelings of sadness and pain we ran away from were still there.

The house was completely vacant and for sale, but the ghosts of my marriage and our last year together remained. My heels clacked on the wood floor and made my every movement echo in the empty house. For a second, the old memories swirled around me like a tornado. "I'm free. This is no longer my life."

But still, like the sadist in me, I explored each room anyway. My ex's office was filled with memories of Play Station game time and the peculiar overstock of golf balls that consumed an entire wall of the book case.

A few feet down the hall there was the spare bath. It was still nicely stenciled with grapevines and a beautiful view of Tuscany.

Continuing my walk down the hall and passing the laundry room, Joseph's fourth birthday party flashed before me. How could I ever forget that party where I scrambled to fill the tiny little water balloons in the sink while the kids howled for more?

And then there was the kitchen. This was my domain. So many memories still filled this room. It's weird how you can stand in an empty room, but the energy there is so present, you have to stop and close your eyes to acknowledge the memories that still reside there, good or bad.

I can still remember stirring soup at the stove when my husband came in screaming about the Discover bill. I can remember taking pictures of my son doing naked play dough at the island. Then there were the countless times we made flubber and homemade cookies here. It was sad to think that none of that would ever take place in the same spot again. Nothing would ever be the same. Nothing. There is real sadness even when the outcome is something you wanted to happen and you knew was right.

Standing in the family room, I pictured our couch still there and remembered the times we laughed and did silly tricks in front of the TV. There were good times too, it wasn't all bad.

My eyes wandered to the swing set sitting in the backyard. Just a peek through the window and the memories replayed in my mind. A flood of tears drenched my face for all the times Joseph and I played flying trapeze out there. The sun streamed through the half-opened blinds. I stood there and cried. Something needed to be released here.

Naturally, my feet carried me upstairs through the remainder of the house. This home was lived in for sure. All the little spots and scratches on the wall were still there. Even the streak of jelly left behind from a gushy ball my son accidentally threw on the ceiling still hung overhead. I smiled.

I walked back to the bottom of the stairs and sat down. Joseph and I used to sit there and look out the window while we waited for one of his friends to arrive.

This had to work. I wanted my marriage to be perfect. I wanted my son to have a perfect family. I wanted to feel loved and adored. I wanted *this* family to work.

My head rested in my hands and tears splashed the hardwood floor. But my memories couldn't overtake me, I pulled myself up. This heaviness and sadness was more than my heart anticipated.

Goosebumps traveled across my body as I passed the guest room that had become my master suite in the past year. The room gave me chills. I hated that room. It was horrible. That was not how it was supposed to be. This was just another one of those situations that made everyone choose.

My son's bathroom soon came to view. It was bright and airy like always. My fingers grazed the old glue marks left behind from the fish stickers we put on the walls together. I sat on the potty and remembered all the bubble baths and the silly stories we used to tell. *Why did it feel like all the good memories would end here? The only thing that ended was the marriage.* But the family went down with the fire as well.

Walking into Joseph's bedroom, memories of his laughter filled the room. I could hear him and his buddies banging around the toys and jumping on the bed. It seemed like months had passed with no laughter coming from his beautiful face…not even a smile. Was it possible that he had left all of his happiness here?

The walls in his room were still painted a shade of blueberry and the adhesive planets held strong. Above my head, a string hung from the ceiling. It used to be home to the infamous Buzz Lightyear.

My office was the next stop. There were marks on the floor from my desks and remnants of silver from my jewelry making. A small jade bead twinkled at me from the floor. I picked it up and tucked it in my pocket, then walked to the master bedroom. The fights, the anger and the resentment that built in the last year of our lives together still lived there.

Of course, there were good memories too. Five years of our life in this house is a long time, not all of it was miserable. Times with my husband weren't all bad. He loved to play with our son and flip him on the bed. They both giggled 'til they cried. After numerous failed rounds of IVF, I remember how my husband held me to ease my overwhelming disappointment. I even remember Joseph's attempt to console me by snuggling with me in bed. Yes, there were comforting and happy moments too, even though they seemed so distant now, and so shattered.

The recollections of our last year in the house continued to swarm around me. The joyous moments gave way to the yelling, the resentment and the pain. Those feelings never left this house and now they were enveloping.

The fight over the crayons the day the movers came screeched in my head. "I fucking hate you," roared from the walls. There was hatred in his eyes while we divided up the Christmas decorations. It was time to go.

The walk downstairs took only seconds. Before leaving, I peered into the bathroom me and Joseph shared towards the end of the divorce.

In the final days leading up to our move, this was my sanctuary. The place where I showered, cried, and purged myself of all that was left of my marriage.

Towards the end, it seemed impossible to finalize a divorce, a move, and take care of my son in the way that he needed.

It was overwhelming to say the least. My eyes never ran out of tears and my heart never ran out of sadness.

Without a doubt, I believed God had me exactly where he needed me to be at that time and at that place. Still, I worried about Joseph, but had to take comfort in knowing God had a plan for him too. I needed all my strength to take care of my baby.

Down the stairs I rushed and ran into the kitchen. I took one last look behind me and cried the ghosts away. With a deep breath, I waived my hand in the air. "Good-bye."

My eyes hurried over the rooms and my lips curved upwards in spite of my grief. "Time to move on girl. Never out of the fight." I whispered.

I stopped in the bathroom and looked at myself in the mirror. I had just been to my stylist and my hair was very spiky and messy. I liked it. I turned on the heel of my new red boot, and reminded myself, "You have the greatest life ever."

Three hours later, Thomas arrived at the door. He was in town for a show, and he was exactly what I needed. We laid out the blankets, lit the candles and put on Thievery Corporation. It was perfect. There were no more ghosts here anymore.

Faith – Hope – Love

In the blackest part of the night
I see nothing…I have no light.
Tears run and sting my eyes
Pain, words and lies.
In the darkest corners of my mind
I am speechless…I am blind.
Drunken, dizzy, breathless and mad
Wanting to run out of sad.
No more wasted tears today
My love for you has melted away;
Cannot take another dark night
Hope is the lamp that lights my life.
Cannot think of yesterday
Faith is my rock today.
Cannot breathe another breath of hate
Love tears down my walls before too late.
In the brightest part of the day
The sun washes fear away;
I feel it warm upon my face
It beckons time to erase.
In the moonlight of the night sky
I am willing the hate to die.
Tomorrow starts a new day
Faith hope and love will stay.

Chapter Eight

Nothing Could Have Prepared Me...

Love

Head First

We made it through the Holidays. *Check*. Everything was unpacked. And several thousand dollars later I had replaced all the things missing after the divorce, up to a new plasma TV, because I could. So I did.

Every day after the divorce was an accomplishment for my son. Nothing could have prepared me for the montage of emotions he felt on a daily basis. He'd wake up and cry. Joseph professed to hate Chicago, to hate me, to hate the divorce, to hate his new school, to hate his new friends, to hate his life…to hate EVERYTHING.

He'd come home from school and cry. He'd eat dinner and cry. He'd get ready for bed and cry. He'd go to bed and cry. He'd wake in the middle of the night and cry.

My response to this scenario was always the same. We prayed together. We always stopped whatever we were doing and prayed. I knew God had a plan to get us through. This moment would pass, but Joseph didn't yet have the capacity to see the bigger picture. We bought a book of bible stories and read them every night. We talked about becoming a man of God. I wanted him to learn to trust in God.

But my heart still broke each time his beautiful face grew sad and cried. The heartbreak he dealt with was more than I bargained for. I would have done anything to take his pain away. And the truth is Joseph was right. This whole experience was shitty.

Needless to say, my heart was dragging. At work, I held back tears. In meetings, I held back tears. In the grocery store, I held back tears. In bed at night, my tears soaked the pillow. This was not my wish for him.

All I could do was pray. I prayed God would give me the words and the wisdom to speak to him. God was testing my faith. We would get through this, but so many moments made it seem impossible.

My faith was the only thing that kept me from losing my mind. I clung desperately to the dog tag that hung loosely around my neck. It was engraved with two things. One side read, "Bring It" and the other side read, "I can do all things through Christ who strengthens me."

These words served as a daily reminder of strength and hope, and I wore it constantly.

Then one day something happened. Something changed. I picked Joseph up from the after school program. He began to cry when we got in the car. My heart was exhausted with the grief. My tears had fallen enough for the both of us.

Driving and staring out the window, I had nothing to say. We got home and he was still crying. Every time he cried, I said the same things over and over.

"OK baby let's pray…let's ask God to come into our hearts and give us happy hearts. Let's ask him to search our hearts for sadness and replace it with love and joy."

Each time, Joseph looked at me and mumbled through his tears, "OK, Mama." We held our hands tight and looked into each others' eyes and prayed to God.

"Joseph, baby, God hears your every prayer and answers every time…you must always have faith in that." I told him every time we finished praying. And every time his only response was, "OK, Mama."

With his lips curled and the moisture from his tears shining on his lips, he always looked at me with all the hope he could muster.

Like each time before, I looked him strong in the eyes and asked, "What is impossible with God?"

"Nothing, Mama. Nothing."

But this time, I didn't have the energy to do it all over again. In between tears, he let the dog out. Because of the mixture of snow and rain, Max's paws were black with mud when he came back in. So there I was.

My son was depressed. He yelled, cried and grabbed at the dog, whom was strangely excited. Max ran all over the house with his blackened paws and left mud EVERYWHERE.

In the meantime, my two cell phones started ringing off the hook. An unfamiliar weight pummeled my chest. Tears filled my eyes. My throat was choked.

I ran down to the basement, sat on the steps and sobbed. The chaos reeled around me. The crying, the barking, the phones, the mud, the chest pain, and my own sadness were more than I could handle.

I dropped to my knees and humbled myself before God. "Lord, give me strength for this situation. Give me an answer and a way out of the pain. Please take the sadness from my Joseph's heart and give it all to me Lord, please. Lay his burdens on me. Lift his tiny soul. Search his heart for sadness and replace it with love and peace."

My tears and my prayers continued until my eyes were nearly swollen shut. But when I finally opened them again, peace warmed over me. I felt calmness linger in the air. Something was happening FOR me and not TO me. I lifted myself up from the steps, dried my tears and took a deep breath.

Nothing changed upstairs. The chaos still roiled. But this day was going to be a new day and an end to whatever this insanity is called.

I walked over to Joseph. He still sat, crying on his bed. I pulled him up, looked him square in the face and said, "Let's get this over with." He looked at me perplexed.

"Get it out of your system. Tell me everything and make sure I hear it. Make sure you say it loud enough."

He obliged. "I hate this Mom. I hate this divorce."

"Yeah. What else?" I got in his face and challenged him.

"I hate my life here in Chicago. I miss our old home."

"OK, KEEP IT COMING." He yelled more.

I yelled right back at him, "Is THAT IT?" He looked stunned at my behavior. And he actually stopped crying just to check in with me. Still, I yelled back at him, "C'mon little man…LET IT OUT. WHAT ELSE YA GOT?"

He yelled back, "I miss my friends and this SUCKS!"

"KEEP IT COMING." This went on and on for several minutes. I provoked him and yelled back at him so he'd know that I wanted it all to come out. And it did. It ALL came out.

My yelling back with him and not at him let him know that it was OK to be angry…mad…sad…but here was the twist. When he was done, when we were both exhausted from yelling, I sat him down and we talked.

"Ya know sweetheart, we've been saying the same things for months now. We have to start looking forward, not back anymore. Let me tell you something about life, SHIT happens to you. It does. Believe it or not, this is not the worst you're ever going to feel in life."

He looked stunned. "Mom, you used the S-H word."

"I know, Sweetie, but here's what…here is what I am going to tell you and this will be one of the most important conversations we will ever have about this so listen real close."

He nodded his head. "Okay."

"When the SHIT happens, it's what you do when it happens that matters most." I paused. "Do you really think God sits in Heaven and wishes for your sadness? Do you think He really enjoys seeing your tears?" My son shook his head.

"NO. God brought you to this and He will get you through this. He ALWAYS DOES, AND HE ALWAYS WILL." I hugged him. "I know divorce is difficult, but you have to have faith. Have faith that God has a good plan for your life and this is only one piece of the puzzle. You will look back at this one day and feel stronger, wiser and better…if you choose. But if you choose to only see what is wrong then you will never find the happiness that God has waiting for you."

"Okay." He said. We dropped to our knees and prayed together.

"Dear God, it's us. We ask you to come into our hearts tonight and put your sweet embrace around us so we can feel your love and your safety from all that we fear. Come into our hearts and search for any sadness and replace it with love and joy. Lord we pray for happy hearts."

We made it through the storm intact, a few broken windows, so to speak, but our hearts were full and our faith was strong.

A few months later Joseph was reading a devotional book he received as a gift and he brought to my attention the following:

> *"I believe in the sun even when it doesn't shine. I believe in love even when it isn't shone. I believe in God even when He doesn't speak," anonymously written on the wall of a concentration camp.*

He looked up at me with tears and said, "Mom, it's like what you tell me about faith, to keep on believing even when things don't seem like they are going to work out."

All I could do was thank God, my prayers were answered. That tiny heart was healing, one day at a time.

Chapter Nine

Thomas...

Head First

So after the indescribable Match.com experience, I decided to throw my world into chance and just meet people the old-fashioned way, face-to-face. This worked well, or so I thought. But in order to do so my lazy ass had to get up off the couch, stop watching reruns of "Sex and the City," and actually meet people.

I made friends, went to some cool places, and met people…lots of people. However, here's the thing about love, or even like: chemistry, chemistry and more chemistry.

The VA-VA-VOOM, the increased heart rate, the sweaty palms. The whole package. Love can't exist without it. So how was it possible that in the entire city of Chicago I couldn't find even one person that I could spark with?

My previous months were spent working on myself and enjoying my solitude, learning, writing and having fun with my gal pals. But was I ready for love? I retraced the graveyard of dates from the previous year and became acutely aware of something profound. Chemistry and love, almost every time…defy logic.

Of the handful of men I chose to be involved with, there are only a few that linger in my mind and even less than that linger in my heart.

Thomas. German, adorable, song writer/musician and invariably always someone else's boyfriend each time we connected. Thomas was 6' 7" with a thin frame and shaggy dark hair that hung in curls around his face. He had baby blue eyes and a perfect smile. He was shy but intense.

It didn't seem logical to want anything real from him. He lived several states from me and ALWAYS had twenty-something, nothing girlfriends.

We were at such different places in life. Thomas lived the life of a musician. He was always on the road, stayed up late at night like a vampire, and survived on pizza and beer. My life was organized, structured, and not obsessive, but I had daily responsibilities that I wasn't sure he could understand. He had roommates. It seemed like he even lived out of his car.

As Thomas and I approached a year of this dance, it became clear to me that having Thomas on the brain was becoming detrimental to any other relationship I might find. There was some internal, deep set reason for my attraction to him. There was also a reason why I was unable to shake him now.

Almost exactly the moment I decided to forget Thomas was when he kept coming to mind. No matter what I was doing, thoughts of him always kept coming up.

We went to Mexico after my son's first school year in Chicago was over. We'd spent enough time crying, enough time talking about divorce, and certainly enough time feeling sad. It was time to get some sand in our toes. A little sunshine and some snorkeling would be great for us.

We checked into a five-star hotel in the Riviera Maya and it was amazing. It was beautiful. But it seemed like EVERY-

ONE was on their honeymoon. Everyone was in love and there were couples everywhere. This was not in the brochure.

Yet my son and I had a wonderful time doing everything we could get into. The time together had worked wonders for us and we loved every minute of it. But with all the thinking time on my hands, thoughts of Thomas crept into my mind over and over. The hotel was one of the most romantic ones I had ever seen. There were places for lovers everywhere. Everywhere I turned there were people in long embraces, stolen kisses, and men and women clinging to each other in the water.

Flashes of Thomas's face interrupted my thoughts. It was ridiculous. Clearly I was out of my mind. Anything was possible. Any emotion was possible for me to feel at this point in time. I could see something in Thomas I wasn't even sure he could see in himself. When Thomas played his music, I could see his talent and his passion. I believed in him, probably more than he believed in himself.

He could be so much more than he was. I don't think anyone really ever spoke any faith into his life. Somehow, strangely, undeniably, I believed that deep inside his boyish exterior was a heart of gold.

The emotions were confusing for both of us. I pushed him away, then I longed for him back. He disappeared at times, then pulled me back in.

In the entire year we danced, we were only intimate a handful of times. It was weird, but at the same time it was powerful.

I needed to move forward or move away. Nothing ever stays the same. There was no logic here, absolutely none. It's not about the material things. It's about people being in two entirely different places in life.

Yet all of this, absolutely ALL of it went right out the window when Thomas came to Chicago to spend the week-end with me.

I was ready to know the answers to my questions. When he arrived at the door, I smiled. His tall, lean frame stood there in all of his vulnerability. The soft curls of his hair framed his face as he smiled nervously. His guitar was tucked almost invisibly behind him as he entered my home.

Our first embrace was awkward and nervous for both of us. He had come with questions and I was prepared to an-swer them. He kissed me immediately.

With very few words and a brief introduction to my sweet little home, we found our way into the bedroom. We slowly and gently peeled off our clothes and stood there naked and vulnerable in front of each other.

In the darkness of that night, on a surprise trip to Chi-cago, the musician met the writer. We saw things in each other that other people couldn't, and for the moment, it was all we needed.

It was what it was. There didn't need to be any rhyme or reason. And THAT was the absolute beauty of it.

When Thomas and I were together we enjoyed each other, we shared with each other, and we rescued each other. We were not meant to be forever, but we would remember each other forever.

Thomas

A Deeper Shade of Gray

Wanting you feels so natural
I didn't ask for this at all;
You are with her,
I am waiting for that sky to fall.

Some say life is black and white
But you have created a whole new color I live each day.
There is no red for love, no blue for pain
Just a deeper shade of gray.

And I want to be with you
Lying in your arms, listening to music;
Sinking deeper into your eyes
Fading quietly into your embrace.
This is crazy madness
You are always on my mind.
I try to shake you... lose you... forget you...
The possibility of your love is unkind

Head First

My heart is like a ticking bomb
This is a dangerous time.
For now, I will tolerate this wait;
The world is hurling but I am fine.

But if I can't get what I need from you
Show me your back and just walk away.
Take your phone and your bullshit
You have colored my world a deeper shade of gray.

In the gray
You are there…almost loving me.
Almost pulling me out from the inside.
Almost securing that space I saved in my heart.
But almost is not where I live, and you have nothing to give.
I am running away from this mess…I am letting you go.
Be with her, or the next one.

Chapter Ten

Chemistry..

Head First

Chemistry makes the heart linger. It makes no sense at times and at other times it can make you crazy out of your mind. After plowing through a million bad dates, and awkward kisses, one guy caught my attention at a local Irish pub on the south side of Chicago. *Of all places, right?*

I'd gone out with a girlfriend and had absolutely no intention of meeting anyone special. In fact, I expected a bar brawl or a cat fight would be the highlight of the evening.

As we slammed shots of tequila followed by our Michelob Ultra's, we were feeling pretty fly. The hot, twenty-something bartender offered a wide variety of shots with names like the Green Monster and the Grape Bomb. It turned out to be quite a night.

While we were there we noticed some guy and his posse of friends walk into the bar. The guy was at least six-foot-four, large frame, probably 280 pounds with long hair, sort of rock star Thomas hair, but a little more like a jock. Clearly he was the best looking guy in the bar. I decided to avoid him at all costs.

He had to be about 30, 32 tops. I was a mere stone's throw away from 35, so what did it matter? Again, my plan was to avoid him.

I was dolled up in a chili pepper red tunic with a criss-cross tank on top. The top had elastic at the bottom that stopped just below my tush and hugged my thighs. There was a draw-string tie just under my breasts. On the front of the tunic was a white, hand painted guitar. My long denim shorts also hugged my thighs and stopped short at the knee. My freshly cut hair was very boy short in the back with long jagged bangs that swept to one side. My eye peeked through the long bangs.

My feet were dressed in four inch black strappy sandals that made my legs look six feet long. My signature accessories complemented the ensemble. I wore my large silver hoop earrings, my single silver dog tag chain, and two hand-carved bracelets. And as always, my fragrance was nothing other than Coco Mademoiselle.

Several trips to the ladies room and his eyes burned through me each time I walked by. I almost stumbled. He seemed to be engrossed in me. Every thirty minutes I walked by him and smiled, not because I wanted to, but because I had to pee! A few hours later he and his friend finally approached me and we made a little chit chat.

He flirted and flipped his hair, a slight turn off for me, but I wasn't going to marry this cat, so it was tolerable.

"Hi, so my friend and I were just wondering what your bracelets say."

I looked at him coyly. "Well, one says, 'Are you a good witch or a bad witch?' And the other one says, 'Do you have any idea who I am?' "

"Are you a good witch or a bad witch?" He asked me.

I smiled and said, "Well man…that depends…"

He looked at me and it was glaringly obvious he had no rebuttal; he turned to his friend in an awkward plea for help.

A little intimidated maybe? Conversation is my thing. I always know how to chat guys up about anything. So he hovered and then I turned away.

I tested a theory I'd concocted with my newly single status. You gotta play a little hard to get. This one is new for me. I'm usually the type of girl to go after what she wants. I don't play games and don't really give a shit what people think.

But turning away and almost wandering off was a way for me to see how much this guy was really into me. Apparently, he was VERY into me because he kept coming back around and around.

I was attracted to him for sure. It was those damn pheromones. But my friend took a disliking to him and sarcastically referred to him as Fabio.

When the bar closed, we were herded out like cattle. "So where are you heading now?" He asked.

"Ummm….it's three in the morning. I am heading to my bed." I said as if it should be obvious.

"Well, can I come over?" He asked without haste.

"Ummm….no…no you cannot come over." In my head I applauded his audacity, but seriously, what was he thinking?

"Well then can I have your phone number so I can call you?"

"OK pal, that would be fine." My intentions weren't to call him, but my play-hard-to-get plan seemed to be working like a charm.

After I made it home he called right away. I refused to see him. Then fifteen minutes later he called again. In another fifteen minutes, he called again and begged me to send him a picture of me in my pajamas. Stern with him I replied, "move on man."

I hung up, thought nothing of it and went to bed. The truth was, had I actually wanted anything to do with this guy, he would not have been so persistent and interested. I'd seen it a million times. So I continued to play out my theory. If a guy is really interested in a girl, then he will persist despite all obstacles.

The next day, an uneventful text from him arrived in my phone. He didn't get a reply from me until an hour or so later. While he waited for my reply, my guy pals did some checking on him. It turned out that he wasn't a man pig. He was really pretty cool and got good remarks from his male peers. His stock rose in my eyes.

I sent him a text with my new cell number, which had recently changed, and now hoped for a return text. Game on. Unfortunately, Fabio didn't return the text. *Had I gone too far? Had my theory proven wrong? Shit…I wasn't very good at this game after all.*

A week later I celebrated my birthday in a large way. AJ and I were prepared to hit the local establishments, which meant we'd be the hottest MILF's those bars had ever seen.

So just as we pulled up to the bar that I had only frequented twice in the past year, I received a text from Fabio that said he was sorry he hadn't reached out sooner, was busy and all. *Blah, blah, blah.* But he said he was very interested in seeing me.

As it turned out, he was already in the bar I was just about to walk in to. *Interesting.* Fabio and I chatted immediately.

It was my birthday and I was celebrating. I wanted everyone to know it. After a round or two of Grape Bombs, I felt reaaaaally great.

Fabio checked me out the entire night. He sent me a text that he wanted to hang out with me.

"Hell yeah," I said. Around 1:00 am, we walked back to my house and stopped periodically to kiss. We held hands and walked under the moonlight.

I wanted to hang out with him…more than once. He had a great look, cool personality and there was a definite chemical attraction.

We made it to my house in a few minutes. Since I had company over for my birthday celebration, we sat outside on my front porch. He pulled me onto his lap and kissed me. Fabio's hair was long. He was a big guy and it felt good to be in his arms.

We kissed like the Titanic was going down and we might not have another day on earth. Seriously, we kissed for over an hour and we said some things. He touched some things. But I was on good behavior.

I drove him to his friend's house around 2:30 am and he grabbed me in the car to make out again. We had another repeat when we got to his friend's house.

My chin was getting chafed and he was really getting aroused. We moved to the couch and he started flipping me around like pizza dough. It was hot, but I'm not really into giving out the candy on the first date. I told him not to trick or treat. He laughed, but he knew what I meant.

The night ended around three in the morning. It was pretty freaking great. I was sure I wanted to see him again and I thought he wanted to see me again.

When I got home I had a big smile. It had indeed been a wonderful birthday. I sat on my bed and went to take off my earrings when I realized I'd left them at his place (the only item that had been removed that night).

"I had an amazing time tonight, thank you, and P.S. you have my earrings." I texted him.

"I had an amazing time too. I'll get the rings to you." He replied back. Game on. There would be a second date with Fabio. *Yeah me.*

I was excited at the thought of seeing him again. But the texting fell off the map, and it was like he disappeared into the Federal Witness Protection Program.

"Not so much," I mumbled to myself as I erased him from my contacts. Fabio fizzled out like a damp fire in December. I replayed the situation over and over in my head. From what I can piece together, I was just too fabulous for him. There is no other conclusion. Well, that's my story and I'm sticking to it.

Three months later I found out Fabio was in a long term relationship with some uneventful girl for the past year. *Fucking dudes.*

Chapter Eleven

I Couldn't Even Make This Stuff Up...

As if I hadn't tortured myself enough with Internet dating, the summer approached and I needed a reason to get off my ass and meet people.

Also, I feared a developing addiction to hanging out at the local bars. That never amounted to anything other than trouble – icky, gross trouble.

So I resurrected my Match.com profile. It must have been something about my profile or pictures that gave off the wrong vibe. My updated profile title became, "I can't believe I shaved my legs for this." Any smart guy could pick up on my disappointment in the previous one hundred dates I suffered through. But then again most guys are not really smart. (No offense, but most of you admit this yourself).

I threw in some swirly good pictures of my trip to Vegas with a gold dress and some strappy sandals. I mixed it all up thinking this approach might drive different results.

You would think the interesting variety of experiences already mentioned would have made me wiser for future date searching. *Not so much.*

Enter Kevin. Kevin had NO pictures on his profile. THIS was my first mistake. *Duh, the no picture guy is NEVER gonna work out.* This was my rookie mistake, but we were just emailing, so it was no great loss.

When he sent me a picture, I was pleasantly surprised. He looked thin with sort of shaggy dark hair. He was Italian maybe, who knows, but he was definitely cute. He was lying on a couch, which looked a bit too country Amish for me, but I wasn't going to be that petty. We started talking and everything seemed pretty good. He seemed normal. He was divorced with two kids. *Blah, blah, blah.* No red flags.

Until…after two weeks of talking (because of scheduling issues), we decided to finally meet mid-day for a quick coffee. I sat in a Starbucks on a summer day in my beautiful black BCBG suit and black leather heals. Very chic and very black. I was in the middle of the work day and he was running late. I ordered my triple espresso and a hot chocolate he requested. Kind of a sissy drink I thought, but I didn't want to judge him. What happened next literally rendered me speechless, dazed and confused.

He sent me a text and requested we go back to my place after the coffee because he wanted to feel my "titties" up. In the same text, he also confessed that he wanted to lick my…ahem…backside. *Ummm…what the fuck?* He was the mayor of Freaktown, population ONE. I should have bolted, but instead had to see what this cat looked like. I thought it was necessary to ride this one out.

I had no response to his text. All my witty banter, my quip replies, and sarcastic rebuttals were of no use to me in that moment. I had nothing.

I was on the phone with a colleague when he walked in. Suddenly her voice fizzled out. Kevin sauntered in with a single, very long stemmed rose in his hand. He was a large dude and he wore a Kool-Aid grin on his face. My eyes darted to the bulky jacket that circled around the center of his abdomen, like a floatation device. The jacket was nice though, especially since it covered up the Blackhawk's jersey that swam underneath.

Kevin made his way over and looked like he was ready for some real fine ass-licking. My train of thought ran off a cliff. I eased the phone away from my ear and hung up on my colleague. My eyes zoned in on the many, many things gone wrong with this visual disturbance standing in front of me.

Sure he resembled Donny Osmond, as he mentioned, if Donny was aging, overweight and skipped his monthly appointment with Just for Men. Kevin's hair sparkled like a barracuda in the sunlight. *And really, what's with the freaking hockey jersey? And where's the guy that weighs 180 pounds wet? Ugh, how dare this mother fucker? The only thing I'd let him lick is the dog shit off the bottom of my shoe.*

I'm sorry. That was rude, but here's the deal. Don't lie to me about this stuff. Don't send me pictures a decade old. Don't lie about your weight. And DON'T attempt to think you're getting some candy on the first date. *Is coffee even a date?*

Don't…don't…don't. Kevin sat across from me without so much as a "thank you" for the $3.00 hot chocolate. He pretended like there wasn't a care in the world.

Nothing came out of my mouth. Not one word. I stared at him in disbelief. I slugged the last of my espresso, stood up and politely excused myself. "You know Kevin, we've been talking for a couple of weeks. And I have to tell you, there's nothing here. I'm sorry."

I took long strides out of there, ready to explode. When I finally got inside my car, I burst out laughing.

Sure, it all seemed so shallow. Maybe he was a hell of a guy. Maybe I could have gotten past the fact that he looked so different than he did in the picture he sent me. Maybe I could've gotten past the Amish couch scene. Possibly.

But the ass licking? *Bleck*. Just the thought of it made me feel filthy and ready for a shower. Who knows how many times he'd used that line. Grrrr…back to the books.

If dating were a matter of statistics, I was ready to turn up the heat. I rolled into another weekend and decided to pull a dude thing. I double booked.

It was time to weed out the wrong men as quickly as possible. Doing this by two's seemed to be more efficient. Date with Jack at nine. And date with Anthony at eleven.

My perfect spot for meeting new, completely blind dates was the Whiskey Bar at the top of the W Hotel. It was so dark in there, it was even possible to mistake someone's race. It was perfect.

At nine, I strolled into the bar with an amazing outfit. It was really worthy of a date that came with a guarantee, but why waste all these beautiful clothes?

I had on a gorgeous mauve sweater that was low in the front, had a slightly cinched waste, and hung down to about mid-thigh. My black suede over-the-knee boots crept up over my skinny jeans. You remember my boots from Crazy Guy? He fizzled, but I sure did those boots proud. I also wore silver chained earrings, multi-strand, that hung down to the top of my shoulders. Even if the dates didn't work out, I was prepared to wing it with this outfit.

Jack's outline appeared in the doorway (again, a VERY dark bar). I could tell my ass was bigger than his. A real turn off. But he was chatty and sweet. We had a decent conversation and a few cocktails. Well, he did most of the talking and I did most of the drinking.

Why was it that the men I selected on the websites were so self-involved? Was I that thorough on my profile that there was nothing left to find out about me?

I wolfed down the pretzels and thought it should have been a dinner date. My stomach grumbled. He went on and on about his stuff. And his breath was a bit munchy, which meant there would be no good night kiss, *as if.*

I sat next to him and smiled because the crunch of the pretzels was so loud in my head. It was like I hit the mute button and I could just see his lips moving…*blah, blah, blah.*

Daydreaming in my own world and laughing at my inner dialogue, the sound of a scratching record brought me back to earth when he said, "Those are great tits. Can I feel them?" Not believing this, I looked down at my watch, stood up, curtsied and cocked my head. "I'm sorry. I have another commitment." Off to the ladies room I went.

Unfazed and ready for date number two, it didn't occur to me that he might not leave the bar and my plans might be foiled.

I peeked out of the ladies room and noticed he was gone. *Check.* I moved to another table in the bar, closer to the window. This bar held one of the most beautiful views of the city. The entire Lakefront and Navy Pier were lit up and looked amazing. Then it occurred to me. The bar staff might actually think I'm hooking. *Shit. Note to self. When double booking in the future, pick ANOTHER bar.*

Anthony came in right at eleven. He was six feet plus, a beautiful build and very handsome. A sigh of relief escaped my mouth. *Another note to self: when double booking DO NOT DRINK MORE THAN TWO MARTINIS before the second date.* I didn't slosh my words, but I did feel the warm buzz of the third dirty martini.

Anthony and I got along famously well, famously enough for a second date. As it turned out, he showed up a little warm and tingly so naturally everything was interesting and funny.

We started making out in the corner of that dark, mysterious bar like there was no tomorrow. His flawless chocolate skin was strangely soft and I unbuttoned a few buttons on his shirt to slide my hand in.

His skin was softer than mine. It caught me off guard a little, but damn it was good. Good fun, nothing else.

We worked up an appetite with our make-out session, so we decided to grab some fish-n-chips at O'Toole's around the corner. It was good. But it never happened again. Sometimes you just gotta leave a good kiss alone. My double booked evening left me exhausted. My lips were chapped for an entire day. The conclusion I came to would be that Internet dating was simply NOT for me. *Do ya think?*

I mean, statistically speaking, when one pillages through enough bad dates she or he would be bound to find someone nice, someone sweet, and someone to have an honest relationship with…*right?* Wrong! It occurred to me that in the world of the Internet, it really prevented people from actually meeting the old-fashioned way. You can put your story on the Internet for people to preview you like a new pair of shoes. Myspace, Facebook, plus all the variety of websites designed for people who just want to "hook up." *Whatever.*

There are so many ways to shop before you buy, that all the mystery is taken out of the connection. And the truth is that people, men and women, fabricate, embellish and flat out lie about their lives, their weight, their jobs…everything. I hated it.

I refused to post my life as a website that people could view while they were "in the mood" for dating, or dare I say, masturbating.

And that's another thing. When did men become so obsessed with the color of our panties? Why does this question seem to surface during the first few conversations? Men were becoming so predictable and disgusting.

Here's how it goes down for guys these days. There is probably some disgusting equivalent for women but, well, just not me.

A guy asks you for your cell phone number, not so he can call you, but so he can send you text messages. Text messaging is the new way of getting to know somebody. We don't need much human contact when we have text messaging. Men have become so much braver as a result of this obsession with the little envelope on the cell phone screen.

Once they have your cell number, they lure you in with their charm and words – bold, courageous and down right horny. That's what happens. Next they want to know what color your panties are. A man would never have the courage to ask this question to your face during the first few conversations. Well, at least not for the most part. The panty color question is usually followed by how sexy we are, how beautiful we are, how badly they want to kiss us…*blah, blah, fucking blah. Puke!*

Sexy leads to raunchy, and raunchy leads to a guy sending you a picture of his erect penis on your cell phone. And here's the thing about getting pictures like that: objects in the window appear larger than they are in real life. PLUS…gross! Who really wants to see the goods all strung out on a picture, on a cell phone, no less? Women are not nearly as visual as men, so save the pictures and just send us some cash to buy a new cell phone once you have rendered our current cell phone unclean with your nasty bean shots.

Okay, I got nothing with the Internet dating thing, but I had a little fun and met some interesting people, but no great loss. I built a network of friends and didn't really worry about meeting anyone special. The truth was I didn't actually have time for a relationship. Sometimes you think you want something, but the reality of your life is very different.

Still, the membership renewed with a few months to go so I patrolled the Match website occasionally. No expectations. No hopes. No cares, just whatever.

It was the middle of summer when I met Dave. Dave was in his late forties and he appeared to have a very solid career, though it was one of those careers where you just smiled and nodded because you had no clue what the person was talking about. His title was something like, International Director for Economical Efficiencies and Intercultural Emissions. I didn't know what the hell he was saying.

Anyway, I agreed to meet Dave Downtown at one of my favorite sushi restaurants. It wasn't as dark as my usual spot, but what the hell?

As soon as Dave walked in the door, I said to myself, "Fuck it. I'm done." Nothing can describe the sense of disappointment when the image you have of someone based on photographs you've seen that seemed safe, is completely shattered when you met them.

First, and in no particular order, Dave was NOT in his late forties, or even fifties, FOR SURE. The evidence for this goes beyond the overall first impression. Allow me to explain. The hair was at best, "old-mannish," very gray, very fluffy, and a bit feathered. This same hair was layered like a thick carpet over his arms and hands. From what I could see, much like glancing at a car wreck, it was plentiful on the chest and perhaps, dare I say the back, too. I even considered the fact that without a shirt, it just might appear that Dave was sporting a little sweater. *Gross…and more gross.*

All of these thoughts occurred to me during the first 30 seconds while he checked me out – up and down. I stared blankly at him and pondered how I might end this early so no one gets hurt, physically. Seriously. Let me refer back to my earlier comments about LYING.

So I sat down across from Dave and I noticed him checking out my legs right down to the nicely painted red toes. This made me uncomfortable, but in my mind I encouraged him to enjoy the view because this would be his last.

My $200 Pepe Jeans from London were virtually paying for themselves, but his repeated glances were disconcerting….*and ummm…gross.*

I slammed down my dirty martini, which was not exactly lady like. The blue cheese olives were amazing. The conversation was unremarkable.

After you've been on enough of these bullshit dates, you actually forget what you told people. It all becomes a blur. It's like a very long sales call that rarely ends in closing the deal.

All this chow-chow made me hungry, but it was too late to order any real food. I got a hankering for a little ice cream. I ordered a delicious dark chocolate treat.

Dave watched me with a blank stare on his face. I believe his tongue was actually hanging out. I offered him a bit of my ice cream with the second spoon that sat untouched. "Noooo, I'm just enjoying watching you eat yours," he mumbled under his breath as if he were already jerking off in his head.

"Check please," I requested of the server, and not nearly soon enough.

I went home and cancelled my subscription…forever and ever and ever. End of story!

Chapter Twelve

There's Always One Man

Head First

There's always one man. One man that seems to raise the bar for all the others you will ever meet. I knew him my whole life. He was right under my nose the entire time; acting like a father when I needed guidance, like a brother when I needed a big shoulder to cry on, and a friend when I needed a good laugh.

He was a Chicago Fireman, Squad One. He was a football coach for a local high school. He was perfect...Joey Perfect (JP). He was the type of guy you just wanted to respect and admire. You had to hug him because of his big broad shoulders. You had to adore him because of his gorgeous blue eyes and charming smile.

I saw him at the Firehouse on Dearborn on more than one occasion. I often parked my car there before heading to Bikram Yoga.

It was a beautiful Saturday afternoon. The seven block walk to Chicago and Wells where my yoga studio is was pleasant. I strolled and bounced with my iPod blaring in my ears. It was the walk back to my car after yoga that was a bit more eventful.

As soon as I arrived at the Firehouse I began to feel dizzy, clammy, and light-headed. The smell of gasoline permeated the air as the Engines and the Ambulances came and went. The overhead sounds of sirens and the repeated calls from dispatch made my ears hurt. I knew that if I didn't sit down and rest I could possibly pass out and I didn't want to cause a scene. JP was working out and so wasn't in the firehouse at the time, and I was embarrassed to have come there. I wanted to run to my car as quickly as possible.

"Hey Gia, you don't look so good," the chief noticed.

"Oh man, I'm not feeling well. I feel like I'm going to pass out," I responded as I wiped my brow, which had grown increasingly moist in the past few minutes.

"I'm getting the cuff, hold on," he insisted

"Don't tell JP I'm here, I'll just sit for a minute and then leave," I begged. Not even a minute later JP was standing over me as the EMT took my blood pressure.

"Hey man, let me take it," JP insisted. "Lemme do it" he barked again.

The EMT was doing just fine. My blood pressure was just fine. I was just fine. JP grabbed the stethoscope and insisted on checking it himself anyway.

I saw the sweat running down his face from working out and I couldn't help but notice the Iolite cross necklace I had made as a gift for him years before. He wore it daily now. It was tarnished but I could tell it was something he never removed. I smiled through my fatigue.

I saw his blue eyes move across the numbers and I couldn't help but love him. "Did you eat before yoga?" he barked at me (which was exactly what I was trying to avoid).

"Not really," I replied, with my head down like a scolded child.

"Don't be a dork, next time, eat something," he ordered.

He commanded the firemen to bring pizza and Gatorade to me on the spot. They moved with haste at his request.

I devoured the pizza as he sat next to me and kept asking every few minutes, "You feeling OK?"

"Yeah JP, I'm good…thank you," I said with a childish grin. I drove home from the firehouse that day as I had many times before, only this time I was feeling so thankful to have this great person in my life. Someone who's love went so deep for me that I knew nothing could change it, stop it, or ever lessen it.

I spent that drive home reflecting on the many other times he came to my rescue. He probably never even knew how often he put a smile on my face.

My first Thanksgiving before my divorce my son was with his Dad and I flew home to Chicago. JP was at the firehouse that day and I couldn't wait to see him. I drove excitedly to the station on Dearborn where he'd been a hero in my eyes and a hero also to his peers for over a decade. I parked my car, ran into the station and saw all of the Fireman gathered around the TV in a postprandial snooze. He was sitting in a chair as I ran to him, and nearly tackled him the minute I saw him.

"JP!!" I shouted with excitement. The smile on his face grew wide, and his eyes lit up.

"What's up Giaaaa?" he responded with equal enthusiasm. There was a place on his neck I had known for years. It felt the same. It smelt the same and it always made me feel ten years old. It was the safest place in the world. There was no doubt how much I loved this man. He tousled my hair and kissed my forehead.

I spent a decade away from him…missing him…needing him, but I was home now. It was time to get to know him again.

There has to be someone in your life you've known forever; someone who's seen you with skinned knees, bad hair, and crooked teeth. Someone who knows you inside and out, and loves you just the same. JP was that someone for me. He was my perfect. He was my brother.

Chapter Thirteen

Reflections Part Two...

Love

Head First

Sometimes you want to remember pain. It feels good to experience it again because it reminds you of your strength, something significant in your life, or the courage it took to see past the sadness.

My father's death lingered in my memory thirteen years later. His journey, his funeral, but most importantly, his life and what it meant to me, as a child and now, as a grown woman.

It was a lazy Sunday afternoon in 1995. My husband and I were debating what we should have for dinner, and what movie we were going to rent. You know, the usual marital dilemmas. Then my mom called. Her voice sounded strained, raspy and sad. She skipped right through the how are you and blurted out, "Your father has a mass in his lungs."

"What?" I waved my arm behind me to find the nearest chair. The news blinded me and my legs became jelly-like. I needed more information. My questions were endless, but I did not cry. It was time to be strong for my dad.

Mom handed the phone to Dad. "I'll be fine kid, don't worry," He said. That was his style. He'd always be fine. He never wanted me to worry.

His voice had been very raspy for the past month and Mom took him in for testing because he also seemed to have lost weight.

"I love you, Dad." I said and hung up the phone. My dad had been through a lot in his time. A World War II Veteran, followed by years of alcoholism and a mid-thigh amputation of his right leg due to surgical complications later in life. He was made tough by these experiences.

I sat in the kitchen with my eyes closed. I was still processing the information in my mind. I kept picturing images of my dad with his smiling blue eyes, wavy dark hair, sitting in his wheel. *Is it possible that he's questioning where God is at this very moment in his life?*

Dad always had his faith no matter what. He carried a tattered prayer book in his pocket and his Rosary beads were ever present, wrapped around his palm, as he quietly pressed the beads between his thumb and index finger. It had been years since he'd been to church because of his limited mobility. He was such a proud man and he would rather not be seen than to fumble with his wheelchair and cause a fuss.

I gave myself permission to cry, but then felt selfish for thinking how it would be so unfair to lose my father so early in life. My promise to Dad was that I'd be there for him to encourage him, to love him, or whatever he needed.

And so his journey began. Testing. More testing and more testing. It was no doubt cancer. It was inoperable and it was, as they said, inevitable that my father was going to die. My brother, mother and I all took turns caring for him through his chemo and radiation treatments. He was never alone at doctor visits either.

I called my father every single day during the remaining days of his life. I never missed a day and never missed an "I love you," or a moment to lift him up in any way possible.

He was so worried about losing his hair and not feeling like a man. I remember pulling up to the house one day and saw him through the windows. The sparse hair stood out and showed the chemo had begun to take its toll.

I smiled big at him and laughed out loud when he handed me a newspaper with his fallen hair stacked on top. I wished I could have worked magic and put it all back in for him. We laughed then and it was refreshing for both of us. He became his old self in that moment.

The chemo not only took all his hair but also his color and his zeal for life. He was tired, sick and weak. On Thanksgiving Day he was so sick he couldn't get out of bed to join the family for dinner. I went to him and rubbed his back because he was in so much pain.

"What do you think Heaven is like?" He asked me with tired eyes. My tears nearly spilled over, but I blinked them back. I loved Dad. He was such a generous and compassionate man. He lay on the bed, vulnerable and sad, while I described Heaven as I saw it.

His back was turned toward me. I gently stroked it with my palm to ease his pain and said, "Dad, I think Heaven is just a place that feels like home. A place where you are surrounded by the people you love and who love you." It took every ounce of strength for me not to cry.

He turned to lie on his back and then said, "I'm sure Mom will find someone good. She deserves a good man, someone better than me."

We laid there together looking up at the ceiling. I didn't know what to say. I was 26 years old and not prepared to handle the thought of loosing my father.

"Dad, don't worry about stuff like that, you have to be strong and take care of yourself," I said. "I love you Dad, get some rest."

"Me too, kid."

The weeks and months that followed were difficult for all of us. My father fought the cancer until the very end, and my mother never left his side. There were times he was so angry, but he never said a word. There were times I knew he was sad, but I never saw a tear. And I know there were times he was crippled with pain, but he never complained. My mother stood by him, carried him, loved him, and believed in him.

I once asked him whether or not he ever prayed and asked, "Why me, God?" His answer summed up his life. Without hesitation he replied, "Why NOT me?"

We all knew it would be Dad's last Christmas. We bought gifts anyway. The lottery tickets he loved so much. The flannel shirt to keep his weakened body warm and the after-shave that was his signature scent.

In the Spring my mother had to move out of the bedroom because the requirements for his care were more than she could give. He had to get a hospital bed. He resented this change. He wanted everything to stay the same. He hated the fact that this had been a burden to her. He hated to inconvenience us because of his illness.

The saddest day of my life came as we prepared for his death and drove to the funeral home to pick out a casket. My brother and I sat in the quiet office with our mother. We listened to the funeral director talk about the details of Dad's burial. I held his favorite white shirt and black sweater. It was the dressiest he had. I clutched his clothes and sobbed uncontrollably. I wanted to get up and yell, "STOP…STOP… He's not dead…HE'S NOT GOING TO DIE…STOP… STOP."

We walked past the rows of caskets. My puffy eyes could barely see a thing through the tears. But they were drawn to the powder blue casket. That was Dad's color. Now on to my next ill-fated task of selecting the church hymns. This was a moment I never imagined would happen, ever.

This church was the same one I had been baptized in, attended eight years of catholic school, and got married in. Everything happened in that church. And now the memory of my father being wheeled up to the altar in a casket would be added to that list.

My mother's birthday and Mother's Day were fast approaching. Dad asked me to go out and get a card for her. This was the first time he had ever cried in front of me. He wanted me to find a card that told her all the words he never said, all the "I love you's" that he had forgotten to say, and the "thank you's" that went unmentioned over the years. The tears shot from his eyes and he hurried to dry them so I wouldn't see.

"Make sure it says all that, OK kid?"

"You bet Dad." He was just like that. That was just his style. He had a big heart. He loved, but didn't always know how to show it.

The following week, things progressed quickly with his illness. Each day he grew more motionless, speechless and lifeless. I spent hours next to him, just holding his hand and talking to him.

His room was hot. It was unseasonably hot for this particular May. The space was musty and smelled of urine and coffee, much like an old hospital room. There were chairs around Dad's bed. We all rotated and took turns to make sure he was never alone. He wasn't eating, or drinking. He just lay in the bed and barely opened his eyes.

His hair started to grow back since he stopped the chemo. It was dark with very little grey and actually looked handsome. He'd love knowing his hair was growing back.

One evening while I sat next to him, he opened his eyes and looked at me. They were still as blue as the sky. He lifted his arms to me and I rushed to him afraid he might be in pain and needed to be moved. Instead, he looked at me, and straight into my heart. Without a blink, or a single shift of his eye he said, "I love you."

It was garbled. His speech had become so mumbled in the past week, but I heard it. I knew those words and I knew how much he loved me. I was his little girl, forever a child in his heart. I hugged his gentle frame and kissed his forehead.

On May 16th I walked into my childhood home and felt the sadness in the air. The house was warm and there was no noise. The nurses were busy taking care of my dad and no one said anything. The air felt heavy and musty. The smell was thick and palpable. Something just felt different and everyone could feel it. Even the dog lay in the corner without moving.

My father spiked a high fever and the nurses were with him in the bedroom, sponging him down and changing his pajamas. Mom was in the bathroom vomiting and my grandmother was sitting in the kitchen crying.

I didn't interrupt the nurses and didn't want to invade his privacy, but flew to him as soon as they were done. Dad's breathing was heavy and fast. He was not responsive. There were no more, "I love you's." There were no more words at all.

My brother was in and out all day, checking on the family and taking care of us. It was a long day. No one really said anything. We all knew.

On May 17th, I went to my father as part of my usual routine before work, but never left for work that day. I stayed with him. I held his hand tightly in my own. It was on this day, the first during his battle with cancer, that I whispered quietly in his ear, "It's Okay. I know you have to go. I love you Dad and I don't want you to suffer any more."

My brother was there too, lying in the bed next to him. He didn't know what to say. He just stared at him. When my mother returned from picking up my grandmother, I knew it was time.

Dad's breathing slowed. It was dramatically slower. The hot May breeze pushed the curtain aside and wandered into the room. God was there. His angel was ready to take my dad and we needed to let go.

The presence of God was there, surrounding my father, ready to take him home. Dad's breath came in quick spurts and then stopped for what seemed like a minute, but then resumed once again. This happened several times.

With his family all around him, his children and wife at his side, he opened his eyes and looked around at us. For a moment, he seemed to be waking up. A glimmer of life came back to him. But then he took one final breath. His body released all tension, his face was freed from pain and his spirit swirled around us. We stood there looking at each other in complete disbelief.

It was one-thirty in the afternoon. People were working, shopping, having babies and my dad just died.

I ran outside to the front yard and just sobbed, "Nooooooooooooo." I dropped to my knees and my head fell into my hands. I had to release the past year of pain, sorrow and heartbreak. My father's body lay lifeless in the bedroom that smelt of urine, and now death. The sadness and the release of this journey to heaven overwhelmed me.

The ambulance arrived hours later. They spent a few minutes alone with my dad and then we stood in awe as they wheeled this man out of his home in a body bag that zippered up the front. It was horrific.

Out of dignity for my father and our family, they kept the bag unzipped at his face. His eyes were half mast and his face was without life or expression. Death resided here now. This home would always be the place where Dad died. He raised his children here, built an addition to the house, remodeled the garage to make a bedroom for his son, and spent countless hours doing his beloved carpentry in the driveway. He was gone now.

I wore a simple black suit to the wake and funeral. On the lapel was a small, single blue carnation that was the color of his eyes, and the color of the sky on that musty day in May. I would never forget it; the day my dad slipped away from us and into God's arms.

Seeing Dad in the casket, that beautiful powder blue I had so carefully selected a few weeks prior was just sickening to my heart. I dragged myself up to the casket and knelt down next to him. My tears were constant. I reached out to put my hand gently on his. His fingernails were dirty, typical of my dad. It made me smile through my tears. His rosary was arranged around his hands as if he were quietly saying it in his sleep. He looked beautiful and peaceful. It was undeniable that death suited him better than cancer.

Friends and family flowed in consistently with their apologies and declarations of love. All I did was stare at them while they pressed me hard in their embrace. It was a blessing when my entire work crew showed up and stood supportively in the back of the room. They made a long line toward the casket to say a proper farewell to the man known only to them as Gia's Dad.

My brother, a state trooper at the time, had a rally of support. My father's funeral procession was like that of a president. There were trails of motorcycles and cars. My father would have been so proud of his son had he seen this. He was infinitely proud of him…always.

The funeral was draining. I'd done enough of the traditional suffering and wanted to get it over with. I needed to grieve in private. We chose a beautiful lot underneath a large Sassafras tree. As we stood around his grave, we all held each other tight. The flag was placed over his coffin in honor of his military duty. I felt a piece of my own death when the casket was lowered into the ground. A piece of my childhood died. A piece of my future died. And a chapter of my life ended.

That night, I stood outside my home and stared at the moon and waited for a shooting star.

To Heaven

To Heaven:
I stand,
To be closer…
My eyes dance
From cloud to cloud.
"Are you there?"…I ask
"ARE YOU THERE?" *louder*
But nothing.
So I wonder…
If I shouted out to you
at the top of my lungs….would you hear me?
If I gazed deeper into the blue sky…would our eyes meet?
If I stretched out my arms to you….would I feel your embrace?
If I knelt at your grave and wept for you…would you feel my pain?
I will always wonder.

Chapter Fourteen

The Miracle of Faith...

Love

Dad was there. I felt him before, but didn't know it was in my power to bring him close to me. It wasn't until my friend Annaliese, my real estate agent and also my intuitionist, awakened something inside me that will live forever. Ann is a fiery German woman who came into my life as my real estate agent but stays in my life as an amazing friend. She was given a powerful gift of intuition. Sounds crazy, even creepy, but this woman could see and feel things that I'd come to understand that she was both accurate and consistent. Knowing her for seven years, I see her gift as nothing short of amazing.

She snapped pictures of my pre-divorce home for a listing brochure, and then came to me and told me things that will live with me for the rest of my life.

"Without a doubt, your father's energy is in this home," Anne said. "There's a distinct white light in the pictures in the master bedroom and in your son's room."

"Really?"

"Yes. He's there. Your father's there and he wants to help you." My heart skipped a beat.

"He's always watching over Joseph. Wow. Your dad's energy is very strong in his room."

"I knew it." Tears drenched my cheeks.

"Gia, his energy is so strong. I can hear him saying that he wants to help you through this. He wants you to know that you aren't alone." I was embraced by relief. It was refreshing to know Dad was with me in this home and in this wretched situation.

Ann taught me how to call for Dad and bring his energy toward my heart. I decided to try it. I raced home to meet my dad. God is so amazing. He gave me a gift few people would ever experience.

Inside the empty house, the strong odor of fresh paint floated downstairs from the bedrooms. The smell was so strong and grew stronger as I ventured into Joseph's room.

I peeked in and hoped to see or feel Dad. Instead, nothing but the stillness of the air greeted me. I walked then to the master bedroom. Inside my former room, I lit a white candle, dropped to my knees and prayed to God.

"Lord, please send my father to me. Please give me a chance to feel him close and to feel his love. Use him to lift my soul from stress, fatigue and worry."

I clutched an old shirt of his. It was his favorite, cornflower blue, almost like his eyes. My tears fell onto the faded, worn material.

"Lord, surround my heart with Dad's love. Use him to soften the heart of my husband and protect my son from pain, from heartbreak and from sadness. Cover Joseph's ears and eyes and shield him from all the fighting and pain around him."

On the floor my body crumpled over this faded blue shirt and rocked slowly back and forth. Dad would come to me. He was here. I imagined him sitting next to God and looking down from heaven at me, as if through a small looking glass. My reflection shone through his eyes. The pain remained with me. Dad could see this, he had to. He had to be pleading with God to help me…his only daughter.

I lifted my eyes after what seemed like an eternity. The smell of paint still permeated the room. The flicker of the candle danced shadows on the wall. While the flame quavered, I wondered if my dad's energy stirred up the air. I believed, I never stopped believing.

Later that night, I tucked my son into bed. Before leaving his room, I placed my hand to my lips and blew a soft kiss into the darkness. "Good night," I whispered to my Dad. Dad was there.

A few hours later I returned to my own bed that I still shared with my estranged husband. We did this only to keep our son from freaking about the pending divorce. I lay down as I did every night, very still, and very close to my end of the bed. Things had gotten so weird at home. This was just another odd ritual that lingered in the pre-divorce process.

I waited and waited for Dad. Nothing. Sleep met me somewhere near midnight. Around three in the morning, I woke up feeling like something was about to happen. I rolled myself over onto my back.

My father's energy washed over me. A weight crossed slowly over my body and almost pushed me deeper into the bed. The bed embraced and relaxed me. All my stress lifted and floated away. My body grew warm and tingly. The feeling was powerful and intense. It felt as if every cell was lifting to the surface of my body. They tingled with energy. In particular, I felt a strong pressure on my right hand. It was as if someone were holding it. It felt like an electric blanket had been placed on me from the neck down to the tip of my toes.

I laid there in the quiet of the night with an unmistakable buzz of energy. Tears ran slowly from my eyes into my hair. It was a bit overwhelming, but very powerful. I didn't want it to end. The feeling lasted for about twenty minutes. It was constant. It never wavered, just like Dad's love. God gave me a great gift that night. It was a gift that would never be forgotten.

The next morning, I felt amazing. I felt like I had a secret to share with everyone. With urgency, my fingers dialed Anne's number. She, of course, was not at all surprised by my experience. She expected it.

"Next time, try to have a conversation with him," She encouraged me.

"That wouldn't be pushing it?"

"Not at all," she replied.

"OK," I said. "I'll try anything at this point."

So the next night, I had a similar experience at roughly the same time, three in the morning. I could hear myself having a conversation with my dad. At first I wasn't sure if it was me creating this dialogue or if he was truly responding to my questions. His voice was similar, but not exactly the same. Again, tears washed over me. *Were you in pain when you were dying?* I needed to know if he suffered. *No.* He said. *I had your love and it took my pain away.* My eyes remained tightly shut but the rush of warm tears fell anyway. *Be your brother's angel,* he said. *Your brother needs you. And don't worry about Joseph, I'll take care of him. Remember, you are never alone. I am always with you.*

After about twenty minutes he slipped away again. I lay there in the darkness, overwhelmed, exhilarated and sad, all at the same time. Everything would be OK. This was all part of my journey.

"Good night, Dad." I said in a soft breath. My words went straight to his heavenly ears.

Over the next few days, I began sharing this experience with my friends. They weren't ready for this. They freaked a little. Mixed reactions were expected, but some of them thought I was losing it.

Over the next few months, I called upon my dad several times. He always came. This became familiar to me and I praised God every day for this gift, even if my loved ones didn't understand.

My family even thought I was crazy, and even more so on a weekend when my mom came to visit. One weekend while my son and ex-husband were on a trip. Mom slept in the guest room and I slept in the master bedroom.

This time, without even lighting the candle and asking for Dad to come to me, he came on his own spiritual will at eight in the morning. He woke me up.

The warm buzz and tingling sensation seemed second nature by this point. It was a very distinct sensation, one that felt great.

Go to your mom, his voice beckoned. *I want to be with her.* After leaving this earth almost eleven years prior, he wanted me to take him to his wife now. *Dad…are you kidding me? She'll think I'm nuts!* He persisted. *I just want to be with her.* This inner dialogue between me and Dad almost made me laugh. And he continued to beg me to go to her.

My thoughts raced back and forth between my own sanity and the absurdity of the entire conversation. THIS, I thought for sure, I had been making up.

I never went to Mom. I never told her, I just went about my day feeling a bit like I disappointed Dad.

Sunday morning came and Dad's energy woke me up again at about 8:30 am. I was in disbelief. I hadn't lit the candle or called for him in any way, but like clockwork, he washed over me. *Please, go to your mom.* He pleaded. OK, two days in a row with this request. This is no accident or coincidence. He needed me to do this for him.

I lifted myself off the bed and felt his extraordinary presence linger with me. Down the hall we walked together. It took everything in me to hold back my laughter.

Mom was going to think I had lost my mind. We walked into the room and heard her sleeping. The floor creaked underneath my feet. Mom woke up, looked at me and wanted to know what was wrong. "Mom, I know you're going to think I'm crazy," I started. "But I can feel Dad's presence with me and he would very much like to be with you right now. Do you mind if I lay down?"

She looked at me and said, "Sweetie, it's OK that you're all grown up and still want to lay with your Mom in bed."

"NO, MOM, it's not like that. Just trust me, please. Dad is here...really." I cuddled up next to her and put my arm across her stomach, much like I did when I was little.

I was a grown woman cuddling up next to Mom in bed. Sadly, it felt good. It felt as safe as it did when I was a kid and ran to her after bad dreams or boo boos. I still fit in that little nook in her neck, and strangely, it felt the same.

Dad's energy moved in step with me. It felt like the three of us were in one embrace. He smiled because he was with his girl again. His love for her was overwhelming. It was sad she couldn't feel him and she didn't believe he was there.

When he slipped away, I continued to lie there and still felt eight years old again. I embraced the moment because it probably would never return. I loved her. She was fiery and crazy, but she taught me how to love.

Maybe Dad wasn't the one who needed the hug. Maybe he did that for me because he knew I would never seek comfort from her like that on my own. Regardless, it was yet another miracle of faith.

Chapter Fifteen

Me Not, Texting You

Love

Head First

After giving what I could to Thomas, things became complicated. Feelings grew deeper and it was all so damn confusing.

Thinking it was the perfect plan, I decided it was time for us to go cold turkey. No more anything. Nothing.

Well, this lasted about a week. On Thursday AJ and I were at Martini Park. We were sloshing down various martinis when his name flashed across my phone as a text message read, "Me…not texting you."

I didn't reply at first, I thought I had to maintain my cool. But then I typed back, "Me…not texting you back." And that was the end of that…no more texting.

It wasn't until early morning on Sunday, that he began to text me with more questions and thoughts. He admitted how much his body missed me. This wasn't surprising. We texted back and forth from four to six in the morning.

"I miss you and I can't let you give me up," his text read.

"But I have to," I responded. This was too much. Our relationship didn't make sense. There was no way I could justify a union between us.

"YOU are beautiful." The text appeared seconds later.

I tried to sleep but couldn't. When the morning arrived, so did a slight headache. But there was a good reason for it. Rewind twelve hours.

I was sitting at a local coffee shop thinking of my "move on from Thomas" plan. This had become my place of Zen and I'd been going there for months to write, and to escape. I was so proud of myself for not texting Thomas. I glanced up from my $10 British Vogue magazine and saw Michael. He was gorgeous. He was twenty-six. He had been running and stopped in for a bottle of water. I had seen him here many times before, and though we stared each other down, we had only a brief introduction over the past six months.

His Under Armour shirt enveloped his muscular chest and arms. Beads of sweat ran down the side of his face. He was stunning.

I sat there in a tank top and shorts with my bare tan legs sprawled out under the table. Nothing but my bright red toes poking out of flip flops.

After noticing each other for months in this very same spot, I had to admit he was getting hard to resist. He stopped on his way out, cocked his head with a shy smile and said, "You wanna grab a drink later?"

"Sure," was all I could say, hoping not to sound too eager. We hadn't even had a conversation, but I knew his age and "story" from others in the coffee shop. We exchanged phone numbers. Game on. I grinned sheepishly and devilishly as I began to thumb mindlessly through the pages of my Vogue magazine, no longer interested in fashion, except for what I would be wearing later.

When Michael sent me a text message later that day, essentially inviting himself over to my place, I grew nervous and excited. I showered and tried on at least three different outfits. I stared excitedly into the mirror and said, "Bring It."

When he arrived at my door he looked adorable. His tall frame shadowed by the night light looked muscular and strong. His eyes danced as he looked me up and down. "Hi," was all he said.

"Hi," I shot right back at him. I invited him in and we sat almost a mile apart on my couch. I offered him a beer which he gladly accepted. I sipped vodka on the rocks, of which I had started at least an hour before he got there.

"So…how is the MBA coming along?" I tried to make small talk.

"Fine." *Apparently he wasn't interested in small talk.*

"Why don't you kiss me?" I asked him feeling vodka bold. He put his beer down and moved in slowly for a kiss. The pouty lips I had stared at for months were now finally planted on mine, and it was as perfect a kiss as I'd imagined. After a long minute he pulled away and smiled.

"You're beautiful," he said pushing the bangs away from my eyes.

"Thank you." I smiled back. Then, without warning, he honked my breast.

"Really?" I giggled at him.

"Nerves," Michael grinned back. Then he shyly asked, "Take your shirt off?" I slipped it off without a second thought. The next two hours were absolute heaven. His tall frame and strong body were eager to please and hungry for me.

"I want to see you again," he said without hesitation. I

tousled his hair as he stood in my doorway.

"We'll see," I didn't want to promise. What could really come of it anyway, right?

Snuggled into my bed, I could smell him on my skin. I fell asleep with a smile. Naturally, by four in the morning when Thomas started texting, my head was bumping a little hard from the glass of vodka and lack of sleep. But I felt great. No regrets. That was an absolutely fun evening. But I digress…so once I decided to get out of bed, there were messages from Thomas waiting for me.

"I can't handle this. I'm addicted to you. You can't give me up. I don't want you to," Thomas had texted. Later in the day the phone buzzed again. Thomas continued to text me.

I had nothing to say. A few minutes later he responded, "Say something." I went silent. I didn't care…I had had enough of wanting him to step up. I had to let him go. I had to. It was just too much work, and I'd been down that road before.

Head First

Falling Into Blackness

I am falling into blackness, spinning, swirling, floating;
Like a feather's journey through the wind,
There is peace here, there is truth.
I am alone, but this will pass, I am sad but this will pass.
I must stand strong, ever believing in the light;
I search for it…I am drawn to it;
Light will lead me, guide me, surround me.
I am falling into blackness, in my mind and in my heart.
There is pain here, but this will pass,
There is sorrow here, but this will pass.
Tomorrow is a new day, I do not understand why I am here
I do not understand why this must take so long
I do not understand why I am alone in this place, but this will pass.
I am falling into blackness;
I see the glimmer of your eyes,
I see the hope in your sky,
As your smile draws wide,
I am ok. I rest in your promise.
Through the blackness I am delivered
Unto the new, unto the blue, unto you.

Chapter Sixteen

It's That Simple...

Love

Head First

I don't know if he'll remember this drive home. There were so many long and short drives where I heard the sweet sound of his voice. He sang at the top of his lungs. My little boy could rap to the Sugar Hill Gang, sing the sweet sounds of Beyonce, and everything in between.

But then there were times when that child of mine let me know I was doing the right thing for him. Times like this voided everything I questioned about myself as a parent.

One night, we were riding home from a friend's house and we had more than an hour left in the car. It was almost eleven at night and we were both tired. I put on my favorite Christian music, which at first, left him a little nonplussed. We listened to a song titled, "You Never Give Up on Me."

And he opened the art journal I gave him. He had the light on as he drew sketches of SpongeBob and Patrick.

His silence was palpable. But then he started singing, softly at first. The love in his voice poured through and built to a crescendo. Joseph sounded so sweet. I did my best to avoid looking at him. I really wanted to see his face, but didn't want to interrupt him.

Then, all of a sudden, his singing just stopped. Silence. I glanced to the backseat behind me and saw tears streaming down his cheeks. His eyes were filled with water and he looked peaceful, not sad.

"Are you okay, sweetie?" I asked him. He turned to the front of the art journal to the place where my note to him was written: "I love you sweet boy…make every page count."

Joseph looked up at me and flipped to the back of his journal. On the back was a picture of a clock with hearts all around it, drawn by my little artist. The picture said: "I love you Mom. I will make every second count."

"I'm not sad, Mom," he looked at me. "And I'm not worried. I'm just so happy to have a mom like you."

We sang together for the rest of the trip. Silently, I thanked God for the work He'd done in our lives. Once again, He'd placed us in the presence of His enormous capacity to surprise and amaze. Tears escaped my eyes just from the thought of how far the two of us had come in the past year. Together, we'd called upon God so many times to rescue us from sadness and to dry our tears. Likewise, we turned to Him with gratitude for all the times He'd moved mountains for us. He lifted the weight of the world from my shoulders each time I fell to my knees. God was always there with rays of light for me.

Once more, I turned to look at my son, to see this little boy who had grown so much in the past year…whose heart had been broken and repaired, whose life had been turned upside down.

There were many things I could now see in him, things that made me proud. Many of these things came out of his sadness, his stress and all the changes that had occurred over the past year.

Needless to say, I was so proud of him. I admired his strength. I admired his courage and I admired his faith.

The dome light of the car illuminated his face. He'd slipped into a deep and peaceful sleep. His heart seemed full and that gave me great peace.

So when people told me he'd be fine and that kids are so resilient, I wanted to tell them to shut up. Their advice almost dismisses the fact that the journey to "fine" is one hell of a treacherous ride. It drains you, it changes you and it redefines who you are.

By now though, I could argue that Joseph was more than fine. He was amazing. But here's what the magic is: it's in faith and believing in the unseen. It's in believing that one day you will wake and not feel sadness. That one day you will not cry and that one day you will find your smile again. It's that simple.

Chapter Seventeen

Packing Up the Ego Bitch

Head First

Aside from getting regular haircuts, brushing my teeth, and the montage of bad dates, the previous year was all about my son and getting him back on his feet.

The end of summer approached, and with one glance in the mirror, I realized that I had evolved further into the woman I was meant to be…the woman I wanted to be.

My body was yoga strong. My mind was sufficiently clear. And my heart was directionally stable.

After months of working with my life coach, I came to realize a few things about my life. In my own subconscious I had created several beliefs that sabotaged my ability to move forward.

One of those beliefs was the careless, even reckless idea that I had escaped my marriage unscarred by the things we dealt with in the marriage. Even crazier was the idea that I had evaded the subsequent trauma of the divorce.

Over time I transferred so much bullshit into my life, just because I did certain things a certain way in my marriage. It was nonsense – absolute nonsense. I developed anxiety if I spent money. I got anxious if I hadn't folded the laundry, or bought all the groceries, or made the bed, or paid all the bills early. I no longer lived in the marriage; instead, the routine of marriage lived in me.

Alberto, my dear friend and life coach taught me how to handle this situation. Not to simplify this process down to a set of three things, because it was much more than that. But there were several "aha" moments which totally caught me by surprise. It was time to acknowledge these ghosts, and it was time to free them.

First, I shattered all the beliefs that held me back – beliefs that subconsciously kept me from being truly free. Second, the "Ego Bitch," as I affectionately referred to her, emerged. She was the voice in my head that told me to feel guilty for doing things that bring me joy. She reminded me of the day when simple pleasures were not allowed. I sent the ego bitch packing and I haven't seen her since.

Finally, I needed to stop judging myself and stop listening to the judgment of others. It's amazing how many people's voices drown out your own. Sure, sometimes they do this out of love, but their judgment can be powerful and it can sink your ship without you even knowing it.

After applying what I learned, I started to see my life was becoming full…full of people…full of love…and full of some pretty exciting things. I was trying new things all the time and meeting new people.

I was living life and love was already in it. Love always surrounded me. For the first time in my life I could actually see myself. I liked her. I liked her a lot.

Chapter Eighteen

The Girl Had It Coming...

Head First

After the perfectly timed run-in at the coffee shop, the breast honk, and the delicious notion that one time would simply not be enough for Michael and me, we decided to continue to see each other.

This went on for months. *I must be crazy. He must be crazy.* But to be honest, when we were together, we were both crazy, and it was fun.

Because our relationship didn't have all the pressure and drama of a normal one, we could just relax and take it in stride. I liked that he wasn't a part of the normal bullshit I dealt with. I liked that he wasn't threatened by me.

Our relationship was all about physical intimacy. When we got together at his loft, or my home, it was playful, fun…sexy. We got together as often as we could.

It was the perfect relationship given the chaos of my life. It was all I really had time for. And it was what it was.

As a few more months passed, I wondered where this was going. Michael and I could never introduce our relationship to the light of day. But still, I grew fonder of him. We grew fonder of each other.

We never cuddled. It just wasn't that way. Things were simple. Until they weren't. Michael's roommate started to put the full court press on me. Every time he saw us together, he always stared at me. It made me nervous.

When Michael and I started to spend a little less time together, his roommate, Christian, really started to move in on me. The Catholic girl in me became restless, nervous and guilt-ridden. There was no denying Christian was cute. He looked a lot like Michael, actually. He was tall, dark and handsome. *Trouble.*

He had two large tattoos on each shoulder blade. They were Egyptian eyes or something like that. It was hard to miss them.

Christian took my phone number from Michael's phone one day and out of the blue, he started texting me about his desires to be with me. I resisted him like the plague and considered myself to be a smart woman. But he was persistent and relentless.

I kept resisting Christian and telling him to leave me alone. This went on for months. The further I pushed him away, the more he pursued me. *Typical, right?*

This proved to be my theory on so many other occasions. Regardless, it was flattering. He was so much like Michael, but yet different in so many ways.

Later in the year, in October, I was working with a client near the campus where Michael lived. We hadn't seen each other in weeks.

Michael had gone out of town to visit his family on the East Coast. I was starting to feel like I should cut bait on the entire situation. Still going about my business, Christian was relentless. He would not take "NO" for an answer. Text after text was about his desire to be with me. Damn, he was good.

I was out at a bar with some friends when Christian walked through the door, out of the blue. I had no idea where he was going and he had no idea that I was there. *SHIT!* I was spinning around in mid-laugh when he walked through the door. The smile on my face froze, and I almost dropped my drink.

I had on a black, off the shoulder sweater with skinny jeans, red Louboutins and my Coco Mademoiselle.

Christian came right over to me like there was no one else in the bar. Our eyes locked and I knew it was "game over."

"I would own you," he said and stared right into my eyes. "Dominate you." I said nothing. I just let my drink slip through my fingers until it landed clumsily on the bar.
That was really unfair. I mean, how was I supposed to respond to that?

I had two Vodkas on the rocks and I felt pretty good. I wanted to leave but Christian wouldn't let me. He physically grabbed my arm so hard it almost hurt, which just turned me on more and more. *Shit. Shit. Shit.*

I didn't ask for this. After I went to the restroom, I stepped out and found him waiting for me at the door. He pushed me against the wall and licked my lips. Nothing more.

I stood there with my mouth open. His taste was on my lips and they were still moist from his tongue. There was no question I was aroused. But I had to find an escape route.

Around two in the morning, I decided to leave while he was in the bathroom. I ran out of there like I'd just robbed a bank.

I jumped in my getaway car – a cab, and headed home.

Moments later, Christian sent me a text that said, "Fuck you, Bitch." *A little harsh.*

I fired back at him and we engaged in text wars until he picked up the phone and called me. We were both hoarse. We were both mad, and I'm still not sure why. We yelled into the phone until I just got tired of it all and hung up. I didn't know where it was all going. It was exhausting.

Yet somehow I figured the whole risk of being with the roommate was part of the heat. In some small way, this was my way of feeling like I wasn't hooked on Michael, even though he was the only person I had been intimate with for a long time.

It all felt so kindergarten-like, really. I had friends who were going through divorces, new jobs, having babies and other real life situations. Yet amidst all the serious issues in life, my biggest concern at the moment was whether or not to cross the road with the roommate. It was kind of refreshing considering all the bullshit I had gone through the previous years. I deserved this delicious dilemma.

I scrubbed my face, put my boxers and tube top on and nestled into bed with LDM. I escaped the madness and felt rather proud of myself. I could use the fantasy, but I could live without the drama.

After about ten minutes of feeling proud of myself, LDM shot off the bed and started barking like we were being robbed. Actually, a robbery would have been better and easier to deal with.

Instead, Christian was at my door and he was staring right at me through the window as I walked towards the top steps. His silhouette was strong in the moonlight. His smile spread across his cheeks. I couldn't think of a single woman who would not have answered the door.

We stood across from each other. There were no words. My first reaction was to slap him in the face. And I did. I clapped him hard on the cheek. He looked stunned and aroused.

"That was for the 'fuck you' comment," I said.

"I'm sorry," he said and pulled me towards him for a kiss. I pushed him away. I didn't want him in my place. I didn't want to be with him. Sure I was attracted to him, that wasn't even the issue. I couldn't help but feel guilty about his relationship with Michael and my own internal conscience that kept telling me to RUN.

But I didn't run. Instead, I pushed him up against the wall. He spun me around and pushed me harder, so hard I slammed into the wall and knocked a picture down.

I slapped him again and he pushed me harder this time. I attempted to punch him but he grabbed my fists and held them tight. He kept trying to pull me close, but I resisted each time and the tension just kept getting stronger and stronger.

I tore his shirt right down the middle and pushed him so hard he almost fell over. He grabbed my waist so hard it almost left bruises. He pulled me in to kiss him. I tried to bite his lip, his nose, anything. He was very aroused and so was I.

We pushed each other around. He was tall and strong, and I was losing the battle. He finally came in hard and grabbed both my arms from swinging. He pulled me in close.

The heat of his body and his breath were hot on my face. We were both breathing hard. He pressed his lips hard on mine. There was nothing more I could do but open my mouth and let him kiss me.

All at once, I felt my body release under his touch. His skin was hot to the touch.

He stood up and I saw his muscular chest, strong shoulders and his smile in the moonlight.

Three hours later, he left and I knew everything was going to be different. It was time to let Michael and Christian go.

I didn't know a single woman who would not have answered the door that evening, but now I had to deal with the aftermath. As predicted, Michael found out. *Of course, right? How could I have thought otherwise?*

With a few burning candles and extra Hail Mary's, I believed I could be forgiven for the whole damn mess. But this seemed like one of those movies where you would have been watching and saying, "Don't do it!"

And the character that you love and feel great about goes for it. Secretly, you're happy for her because of all the bullshit she's been dealing with before this. But under your breath you say, "Damn… now what?"

That was me. And it got a little messy for sure. I made a mistake and should have had my head in a better place. Michael and I came out just fine. He was mad and hurt, but it made us evaluate what we had going on.

I no longer went to his place. We took a break, but then slowly, over the next few months we just couldn't resist being away from each other. It was simple, and that was all I wanted at the moment.

Strangely, that night made us realize we really did like each other even though having a "real" relationship was out of the question. We wanted to be with each other. And so we did, for the next year and a half.

I think it made us both realize we weren't just in it for the sex. As strange as it might have sounded, we really did care for each other. As much as we both wanted to separate the sex and feelings, the feelings just crept in.

I never pretended he was more than he was. It was all good. Oh…I probably should have mentioned they were brothers. Twins. Identical.

Chapter Nineteen

It Hurts Every Time...

Love

Head First

The one year anniversary of my divorce was approaching. And what a hell of a year it had been. Lots of laughs and good times, and certainly my relationship with Michael had been delicious.

But it took me this long to actually feel free, to feel like myself again. And I was being selfish. Granted, Joseph always came first, but when he was with his Dad, I just wanted to learn as much about myself as possible.

I was having a blast. However, there was one thing, one teeny tiny thing that somehow seemed to keep me from complete happiness – time away from my son. I was in a very generous child "sharing" arrangement, which to me was absolute bullshit considering the number of things during his life that were not "shared." Like the millions of poopy diapers, baths and bedtime stories. But I digress. . . .

Every other weekend was a long weekend where my son went to his Dad's from Wednesday through Sunday. This was a killer. I spent the first nine months of this weekend in the fetal position crying on my bed. It hurt so much. I felt empty.

As time passed, I learned to keep myself busy with my Bikram Yoga, or my writing, or making jewelry. But in the midst of the endless amount of people and things to fill my time with, there was still one small problem. All I wanted was my son and his sweet little eyes and soft little cheeks.

You never really understand silence until you have a child in your home, and then they leave. They take the noise with them. When they're gone, you can almost hear the air move.

It's stagnant as if the energy has stopped moving. I did get better at the crying part, but there were other little twists to life after divorce. When my son started baseball I had the weird dynamic of not being with him before, or sometimes after a game because it was "Dad's day."

It broke my heart the way he sometimes detached himself from me because of his dad's reaction. I felt his heart run to me and put his arms around me, but very often he was shy around me in these situations.

There was nothing worse than seeing the child you carried in your belly for nine months treat you like a stranger. But that's how it felt sometimes.

When the game ended, I hugged him tight and shoved my sunglasses over my eyes so no one saw my tears as I walked away. With my head down and my heart sinking, I climbed into the car as quickly as I could and cried. Sometimes it took hours to feel better.

I always thought I'd be the type of mother who never misses anything: be there for all the firsts, all the boo-boos, and all the heartbreaks and disappointments. But with divorce, you just can't. You can't have it all. You can't be there for it all, and it hurts.

It was weird how sometimes I talked with my son and he told me things I knew nothing about in his life. Places he went or people he knew that I didn't know. It seemed so unfair to miss any of that. At times these events made me feel disconnected from him, even downright sad.

In the middle of crying one day, another mother came up to comfort me. She looked at me and said, "I've been divorced for four years, and that look you have on your face, and the way you walk away to your car…well…it never ends." I wiped my tears. With sadness in her eyes she said, "It hurts every time."

I decided to take up this subject with my life coach. After all, this feeling was so overwhelming that it interfered with other things in my life. It was time for a new perspective.

The deal breaker occurred on a long, long Friday before Halloween. I had terminated my third employee in three weeks. This involved a shit load of emotional chow-chow and took over an hour as the employee seemed to not understand the words "you're fired" followed by, "this decision is final and irreversible."

Then, after that was a trip to my annual gyne appointment with a new physician. He was a large, older gentleman with fingers the size of Kielbasa sausages. Needless to say I felt completely violated by the two-finger pelvic, followed by a courtesy rectal exam, which gave a whole new meaning to "the shocker." Yes, I was living the dream, baby.

As if the day wasn't draining enough, I volunteered for a Halloween event at my son's school and was completely blindsided when my ex showed up with his new girlfriend and two kids in tow.

I didn't care that he was dating. In fact, I'd hoped it would soften him up. But I hadn't met her yet, so clearly I knew what I would be doing that night. By 10:00 p.m., I was ready for an entire bottle of wine. Ben & Jerry's would have been too cliché, but it sounded pretty damn good. Instead I opted for a long walk with my LDM, who was really the only unconditional love I could find these days. He was warm, loving, full of energy, and was always, always excited to see me.

So I had the iPod all set to my "sad gal music." I set off to prepare for a good cry and some well needed solitude. But before I could adjust the volume, I ran into Jackie. She was my neighbor with whom I had become good friends. She was blonde with green eyes and full of passion for life. She had great energy, which is why we got along so well.

She lived two doors down with one of my favorite families on the block. I can still remember meeting her twin brothers, both of whom served in the military. They were good looking men, but young. I laughed at the irony of my current situation. *Holy shit, are you kidding me?*

Jackie was cute because she actually clapped when she saw me. She grabbed some smokes and took a walk with Max and I. It was nice. She saved me from crying. She was my angel that night.

We talked about some real stupid stuff – mostly sex – like we always did. She had a very interesting sex life with her boyfriend and it kept me on my toes. I wasn't ready to share my recent adventures with her, but it was always good to hear what the kids were up to these days. Jackie and I laughed a lot that night. It was perfect timing, just what I needed.

Yet the pain of missing Joseph had not subsided. Nothing could fill the void, and I didn't want it to. Every time he was away for these long weekends with his dad, it felt like something was missing.

So I told my life coach, Alberto, we could move on from my work issues. I got a whole new set of problems eating at my inner core.

Alberto is Chilean, with an adorable accent that was comforting and loving. He was all about me. But then again, he WAS my life coach. We talked at great length about how I felt during these long periods of time without my son. We discussed this situation through various different lenses.

The conclusion of our session was the following: the love I have for my son is greater than any barrier of time or distance. The bond we have can never be broken by circumstance or choice…it is forever.

Alberto taught me to visualize the love I have for my little boy. I told him that when I think of Joseph, I visualize my heart as a jar that opens by turning the top lid, just like a regular jar. When the jar is open, you can see the brightest light emanate from the inside. The light was so bright you almost have to turn your eyes away. The light shoots out of the jar and you can feel the warmth of the light, like getting close to a hot light bulb. It shoots out and the heat and light warms my entire body. Each time I miss my son I visualized this love, this jar of light and warmth. When I do this I feel my body release all the stress and my heart fills with happiness.

A smile stretches across my face and I know I'll be alright. See, our love is always there, always in my heart.

One day soon after, Joseph and I enjoyed our usual day of fun. We rode bikes along the beaches of Lake Shore Drive. It was a glorious day and the last of the sunshine, or so we thought.

We rode for miles and sang our favorite songs. We stopped for Italian Ice and sat under a tree while we watched people coming and going. We ate dinner at his favorite restaurant, Gino's East Pizza on Superior Street. We took the crayons and left our signatures on various walls and enjoyed the graffiti.

As we waited for our pizza, I watched him talking in his usual animated way. We were sitting on the terrace on the second floor. It was a beautiful Chicago evening. It was getting a little crisp, and the sun was a burnt orange across the skyline.

I couldn't help but take a deep breath and smile. *Thank you, God. I made it home. I'm back to my roots and this feels amazing.*

I worked at the hospital a few blocks away during my college days. I ate at this very same restaurant during my teens and I walked these streets a million times.

The look on Joseph's face made me smile. I couldn't help but grab his little hands and wrap them in my own. I brought them to my lips and kissed them gently.

I just looked at him with the warmest love I had. We were debating a very interesting topic: if colors had personalities, what would they look like as people? We determined that Mr. Orange would be fat, bald and a real funny guy. Mrs. Purple would have an outgoing personality and a very beautiful smile.

Before we could get through the rainbow of colors I couldn't help but look at him and smile so big, it brought tears to my eyes. We locked eyes and I knew there was something I had to tell him.

He looked worried. "Mom are you okay?"

"Yes, sweetheart, but I need to tell you something very special." To him this seemed a reasonable excuse to shift from our topic of color personalities.

"I love you…and Mom is going to tell you something so important that I don't want you to EVER forget it okay?" He looked at me with his big brown eyes and leaned in for the news.

"I know how we can make it all feel better when we can't be together. Because sometimes I do get sad when you're away, but I don't want you to ever be worried about me or feel sorry for me. I have a secret that helps me and I can tell you what it is if you want it."

"Yes Mom, I want the secret." I described my heart as a jar, closed tightly in my chest. "When I miss you so much it hurts, I let a little love out of my heart to warm my body."

Then I told him about the beautiful light shooting from the jar, swirling all around me and heating up my memory and making the sadness disappear.

As I described this to him, his eyes filled with tears, and his bottom lip quivered. Tears fell from his eyes and splashed on the table below him.

"What do you think about all this?" I asked him.

He looked at me with intent and sophistication and leaned in close to my face. "Mom, would this light come out of my toes when I think of you?"

I grabbed his cheeks in my hands, kissed him on the nose and said, "Yes, honey. It will even come out of your nose!"

That was all he needed to hear – enough love from Mom that it comes out of his nose!

And THAT was all I needed to hear. It's not fail-proof, but it's a hell of a lot better than sitting around crying.

But the truth is, it still hurt…every time. She was right. Life is about choices.

Chapter Twenty

Head First

The night before my second official Thanksgiving as a divorcee, I went to bed a little depressed. It didn't start out that way. After all, there was no real reason to be depressed.

My career was amazing. My social life was growing and filled with friends from every age and walk of life. I was in incredible shape, good health, and was surrounded by people who loved me. There was nothing for me to complain about.

For the moment, I had everything I wanted. A romantic relationship was not front and center in my mind. There was too much of me, way too much of me to take care of at the moment. And I loved every minute of it.

However, some of my single friends did not love it. Somehow their creepy insecurities, false beliefs, and undeniable depression rubbed off on me. BULLSHIT!

This was nonsense and I refused to let it take my joy. I didn't feel the need to apologize for being amazing and successful. It's not my fault that some men don't recognize wonderful until it's too late….or some not at all. But regardless, the pressure of my friends' conundrum swallowed me up.

Thankfully, and amazingly timed, I woke on Thanksgiving morning with a completely different attitude.

Joseph slept in the bed with me because of the family visit, which rendered the only other bedroom the "guest" room. Like clockwork, he woke up at seven-thirty, just as the sun was beginning to beam through the shades.

Our seventy-five pound dog, Max, was spread out across the bottom of the bed. And my son was stuck to the middle because of his fear of monsters under the bed. Between the two of them, I could barely keep a cheek on the bed.

At any rate, I felt Joseph lean over to me. He pushed my hair aside from my face and slowly woke me up. At first he just looked at me with his adorable brown eyes. Then he put his lips on my ear and whispered, "Happy Thanksgiving Mom."

"You know what's so great about you, Mom?"

"No," I said. "Tell me."

A small smile grew on his lips. "You never let me down Mom. You always take care of me and you never miss anything in my life." I cried immediately. He was a little genius. He was the most soulful little person I had ever met.

He took a finger and dried the tears from my morning eyes. A moment later he leapt out of bed to get the Wii going. It's amazing how touching those few words were to me. I'd probably remember them for life. And he was off to play Mario Kart. It was cute.

I sat up in my bed pretty stunned. He had set the tone for the entire day with one single sentence. He put it all into perspective. I would not allow the negative thoughts from my pre-slumber state of weirdness to take root.

I sat and stared around my room. I closed my eyes and prayed to God. The words came so easily for me. I had so much to be thankful for.

There was no question in my mind that a healthy dose of "thank you" was what I needed. Giving praise for all the wonderful things in my life, all that I had come through in the past year.

"Thank You Lord for this day and for the gift of this sweet little boy who guides me, who keeps me grounded. Thank You for this life. I am so blessed. I am surrounded by Your goodness and mercy. Thank You for all that you have allowed me to have here. Thank You for the opportunity to be a blessing to others. Thank You that You live in my heart and with Your love I can do all things."

I got out of bed and went over to my mom who sat on the couch with Joseph. "I love you," I said and put my arms around her. I squeezed her tight. Tears came down my eyes and were pressed between our cheeks. I just needed her to feel my love.

The day progressed nicely. There was food. There was wine. There was more food and then there was more wine. To prevent myself from falling asleep after over consuming both, I decided we needed a little music, so I cranked up the jams with "Sexbomb" by Tom Jones. I danced around the house and rotated through the family.

Joseph was familiar with my erratic and predictably crazy behavior so he was just smiling and dancing with me. I twirled my Mom around and she was laughing and spinning. I pulled my ninety-three-year-old Gram up off the couch, gave her temporary relief of her oxygen, and she was shaking her arms and butt (a little like the chicken dance). But hey, Gram was getting down and we were all having a good time.

A little later, I finished the holiday clean up. My Gram smiled and walked up to me. She was actually so tiny, she barely reached my breasts. But she came over and put her arms around me and rested her head on my pillows.

I dried my hands and returned the embrace. She looked up at me and said, "I just love being with you." Her smile was so innocent and sweet. Her eyes were full of love and gratitude.

"I love being with you too Gram," I squeezed her.

Holding her in my arms, thinking about her and the rest of my family, I couldn't help but think about how much God had blessed me. I've experienced the richness of love, gratitude, and eternal significance to another human being.

What a day to cherish forever. I felt sorry for my friends who couldn't accept their own truths. I could only hope they would understand the power of faith, of never giving up on the belief that there is a magnificent plan for each of us. All things happen in God's perfect timing.

Chapter Twenty-One

Christmastime...

Love

Head First

I sat on my plush, warm couch, nestled in a pile of warm, fuzzy blankets. The once roaring fire was down to orange embers. The last of my Bloody Mary tasted salty and made me bloated. The half-nibbled inch-long piece of celery looked a little bloated too from floating around in the frothy red goodness that was previously my new best friend.

And of course, a well-chosen movie topped the evening…"The Wedding Planner." *Lovely.*

About two hours ago, the first Bloody Mary left a delicious warm buzz. And the olives, which replaced dinner, were outstanding.

About four hours ago, this was exactly what I needed. Four hours ago, I walked away from my child on Christmas Eve for the first time in eight years. For the first time, I was not able to track Santa, to put out the cookies and await the eager morning ritual of tearing into the presents. No, this was not "MY year," it was Dad's.

Even though I would see my little cherub on Christmas Day at 2:00 p.m., it just felt like something was missing…those sweet little eyes staring up at me at bedtime with all the wishes in the world. No, I did not see those eyes tonight. And quite frankly, it was killing me.

It was my brilliant idea to attend Christmas Mass with my ex. I thought it would do Joseph some good to see us both together, without the arguments or nasty exchanges of text messages. So when Mass was over, he turned toward his dad with all the excitement of Christmas Eve. I kissed him on the cheek, turned on my heel and went to my car. We exchanged lots of hugs and kisses and walked out of the building. The bitter cold weather in Chicago made the pavement slippery and the air felt like an arctic wind chill.

I walked back to my car without gloves. My boots did a clicking and sliding combination, all while I was trying not to cry. In mid-trot on the ice, I kept saying to myself, "I am NOT gonna cry. I am NOT gonna cry." But of course, while saying it, I was crying.

I finally made it to my car, sat there and stared at the wheel. I just wanted to run away.

My tears fled freely, loosely. They jumped from my eyes and almost kept me completely distracted from the beeping of my ex who had pulled up beside me. *Fuck. Now what do I do?*

It was too late to hide the evidence. I dotted my fingers to my eyes, took a big sniff and rolled the window down slightly.

"What's up?" I asked.

"Joseph just wanted to say good bye again."

"Hi, baby. Mommy loves you." Joseph could see my eyes and he was worried.

"Wow…it's so cold outside, it's making my contacts water." *Done, he believed it.*

So it was off to bed, me and my Loveable Dog Max, who had bad gas that night. If the Bloody Marys didn't gag me, I was sure his ass pointing at my face would actually wake me from my slumber…and then gag me. Sweet Dreams.

Chapter Twenty-Two

Christmastime Part Deux…

It was now approximately forty-eight hours since I last sat quietly on my couch. I described those hours as a Category 5 hurricane. My house was truly the evidence of a natural disaster.

Christmas morning came and the presents were ready. The milk and cookies were eaten and the stockings were hung. But it was 9:00 a.m. and I was still in bed with my LDM. I was not interested in getting up.

There was no little boy running into my room declaring Santa had come. The only person barging through my door was my mom.

"Get your sad ass out of bed and join the living." She said. I love that woman. She didn't put up with my shit. No pity parties allowed when she was around.

When I did finally speak to Joseph, it was just after nine. I was secretly pissed that my ex didn't encourage him to call sooner, but I should have stopped expecting so much, right?

Anyway, the enthusiasm in his voice was all I needed to hear. It was the birth of Jesus and like any other child all he could think about was the presents. *I had to keep working on that.*

He was happy about his loot and excited to be coming home to mom for more presents. He walked in right at two in the afternoon with a huge smile spread across his face. *It can still feel like Christmas morning in the afternoon.*

My son tore through the presents with the excitement of an eight-year-old. He flew through the paper in search of more and more toys. He found them all and was delighted with Santa's generosity. Most of all, he was thrilled with his number one gift. Guitar Hero: World Tour. That's right, GAME ON. Guitar Hero was going to be great fun for both of us, hours and hours of fun.

Not long after that, my mom, brother and the crew came over. The kids, the presents, the food, the pina coladas…the rest is a blur. Twenty-four hours later, Joseph was back at his dad's.

And as I sat then, with the stillness in the air, the energy of the moment swirled around me. The air stood still to give it room. I loved this moment – and I hated this moment.

All around me were tiny bits of forgotten wrapping paper, Lego's, clothes with tags, and the infamous drum set and guitar of Guitar Hero. We enjoyed it and jammed for hours. But I hated that I was alone again and without Joseph. It hurt every time.

I sat on the couch for about an hour. I watched the room and felt sad and empty. I made a few calls, but each friend I reached out to was out with their family, or they had visitors from out of town.

It only reminded me of my loneliness without Joseph, and made me feel like shit. I choked on my tears and with a fake smile plastered on my face, I hung up.

No one knew what to say really. They were all very satisfied with their married lives. Yet, I was caught between pseudo-singledom and single-momdom. *No, you won't find those words in Webster's Dictionary.* So, I did what always worked. I dragged my sorry ass off the couch, threw my dog in the crate and headed for Bikram Yoga. The sadistic torture of the temperature, the twisting, and the near fainting was all I needed to eject myself from my crashing plane of pity. It was time to be hurled back into reality. My hope was for sanity.

Not too many Yogis' were at this Friday's 5:30 class. Apparently everyone else had exciting plans. Yoga worked, as always. My ability to think of anything other than not fainting or not puking was impossible when torturing myself with Bikram. My mind had a chance to wander into complete exhaustion by the time it was over.

The best part about Bikram Yoga is being done with it. After class, I was completely shower wet, as usual. I bundled my wet self back into my hoody sweatshirt and parka to face the Chicago winter and mull over my options for the evening.

I strolled down Wells Street with my hood slumped low over my eyes and my "Muppet gloves" as I liked to call them. My phone beeped with new messages that came in during my class. I fumbled with the gloves to check them.

There was a message from Thomas that said he was passing through Chicago traveling and his flight was cancelled. I phoned him immediately, gave him my address and had him take a cab to my place. I raced home to shower and tidy up the natural disaster area.

When Thomas arrived it was near 10:00 p.m. and I managed to pull it all together before he got there. It'd been about six months since we'd seen each other. We had what we had when we had it. That was that. But there was a deeper connection between us that we both knew would last forever.

He stood tall in my doorway. His hair was shorter, but his smile was the same. His blue eyes sparkled. He was tired. It had been a long day traveling but I suspected God sent him along as a little angel for me, and maybe he needed an angel too. We hugged for a long time.

It was so nice and so unexpected to see him. We headed out for a few drinks to decompress and get reacquainted. We lay together for hours. It was sweeter and even more intense than the last time. We were together and it was just perfect. It was just what I needed, just what I wanted.

After sleeping for only a few hours he gently woke me and made love to me again. It was soft, it was sensual. Outside it was thundering and rain was pouring down, which was odd for December in Chicago. But all I could hear was his breath on my neck and his heart beating on my chest.

An hour later we were off to the airport. We said very little on the drive, we just enjoyed the silence of each other.

When I returned home it was once again silent, a feeling I was becoming all too familiar with. I thought about this for awhile.

Why was it during this time that I allowed it all to come out? But then I realized there is nothing wrong with silence. Silence brings us closer to ourselves – to who we really are. It is in the silence that we can hear the truth. It is there that we can really savor the deliciousness of life, and etch the most perfect memories onto our hearts. It is there that we can feel pain, in private, in honesty, and courage with ourselves.

I was free in the silence. I was with God in the silence. I have no fear of being there. An interesting thirty-six hours for sure.

Chapter Twenty-Three

Right Now...

In the stillness of that very moment I felt my life changing. Each molecule was changing, each breath was re-charging and each heartbeat was glowing. It was time to begin again.

It was time to stop the nonsense and focus on the significant. Me. I was significant. Everything had a right order to it, and perfect timing to affect people and events in my life. I wanted this to shine through.

In exchange for the vision, I offered up the truth. I exposed my flaws and believed that I could be reborn after learning from my mistakes. No more chance or happenstance. Direct intention and intentional directness. This energy and this force worked through me and enlightened my path and changed me forever.

I would not fear the darkness, but more importantly, I would not fear the light. In the light, I was ONE. In the light, I was fulfilled. In the light, I was all I was intended to be. In the light…I had eternal significance.

No more ego and no more heady logic. There was only love, clear and present love. It was revealed to me and it spoke to my heart. I would not be guided by judgment, from myself or others. I would not do things just because they made sense. Rather, I would be guided by my heart, following my dreams and creating real happiness.

So I accepted the Divine order of my life and the solitude of my present state of being. Physically, I was alone but I knew that spiritually, I was never alone. Spiritually, I learned more about me. My soul was one of a kind and could not be diminished in any way. Through my eyes, I can only dream. Through my lips, I can deliver words of love. And with my hands, I can create in a way that my soul was given charge to carry out.

I accepted things…my life choices…my mistakes. I gave Him praise for all lessons, for all people and for all the love that had come and gone. I released the toxins and let go of all the things that pulled me into darkness. I let go of everything that darkened my soul.

I honored the state of mind that caused my sadness. I acknowledged that sometimes I could not hear God. I accepted that this journey was not my own. I recognized that I needed to be more honest. I understood that loneliness was a state of mind and not of my spiritual soul. I acknowledged that the world needs more love, and I needed to do it better.

Head First

Escaping the Noise

Standing on a street with the city swirling around me
My thoughts and words are one.
Nothing is clear and everything is hazy
I am desperate for the world to come undone.
I raise my eyes to the city lights
My hands cover my ears and I turn from side-to-side;
My mind races with the noise around me
As a world of truth and lies collide.
We are running through this world so fast
Talking, screaming, yelling, hot into the air;
I am blocking out the noise for once
Shutting down all systems for repair.
Sex, Politics, Love and Religion
Everyone has so many opinions and words;
We are full of shit. . .it's just a matter of time
I will see you stripped naked and unheard.
I am escaping all the nonsense, all the noise
Friend, catch me, find me if you dare;
I am in the forest, I am in the breeze
Rising above all that ever made me care.
In the moonlight of the night sky
I am willing the hate to die;
Tomorrow starts a new day.

Chapter Twenty-Four

About Love...

Head First

I dropped Joseph off at his dad's and returned home. I sat down in my cozy chair. LDM followed suit and sat in front of my feet. I rubbed his back, while my mind stayed occupied with thoughts of people, relationships and the holidays.

There is something about the holidays that make everyone think about the things they don't have, why is that? Men want women. Women want men. Women want babies. Women want husbands and men want wives and big toys. But the point is – we look around at what everyone else has and consider our lives deficient – like something is missing.

But I really don't think that's the case. We're not missing anything that we didn't intentionally leave behind in our past; or perhaps deflect out of fear in our present, or push out of the way for our future.

Everything we have in our lives is exactly what we planned. Everything we want in life is just outside of our comfort zone. Sounds self-righteous, right? But really, all this whining kills me.

Sure, I got sad. Sure, I felt lonely sometimes. But being alone doesn't make you lonely.

Truthfully, our lives are exactly as we planned. Sometimes we go through seasons that are not so nice. Seasons of snow and rain that make us feel sad and depressed. Times when the world is so heavy, that every breath seems impossible and unthinkably difficult. However, the things we want in life are available to all of us. They are within the reach of our fingers, if we just STRETCH. But that's the problem, people don't want to stretch and grow – to reach beyond their comfort zone. And hey, I'm full of a lot of bullshit too, because I'm not exactly where I wanted to be. But I'm getting there. One day at a time.

So, back to my story. I dragged myself around the house. It was Friday night and I had no real plans. There was nothing at all that really excited me. After all the food and wine I'd consumed lately, plus the tub of Ben & Jerry's I scarfed down the day before, my body felt fat. So, it was time for more of my beloved Bikram Yoga.

Bikram Yoga was the equivalent of stuffing yourself into a sauna for 90 minutes, almost naked, contorting your body into 26 positions. Wait, that's not the equivalent. That's the actual class…105 degrees, 26 positions, 90 minutes. I had grown addicted to it. Need I say more? Clearly I'm sadistic.

This is the most difficult exercise I've ever participated in. It's always a matter of mind over body. I spent half the class just hoping I didn't throw up. WOW, is all I can say about the entire experience.

At any rate, I hauled my ass out of there to get to the 7:30 p.m. class. Since I was a little early, I stopped at my favorite clothing store, BCBG. Shit! Thirteen hundred dollars later, I raced to get to my class. *Seriously, with a fifty percent off sale, how could I resist? I'm only human.*

Ninety minutes later, my body was soaked. I hadn't thrown up and I felt pretty frickin' great. The class was small because, well, it was Friday night at 7:30, and I suspected most people had plans. I had NONE but I was okay with that. In fact, sometimes no plans were the best plans ever.

My phone blew up with a variety of uninteresting offers. I passed. Instead, I went home and blasted the music (a little Radiohead, Eminem, and, of course, I had to bounce to a little Tom Jones, my new retro favorite).

Afterwards I took a long, hot shower and indulged in my favorite Lush products. There was no sunshine without my Buffy Bar.

I stepped out feeling fabulous, amazing, and very, very hungry. I wrapped my glistening body in a soft as velvet robe, and for some reason decided to eat my toast while sitting on the counter. *Typical single person dinner, I know.* It wasn't because I don't own chairs, but I did it because I could. Because I could see out the window better. Because it seemed like something a child would do. Because I wanted my feet to dangle. Anyway, who cares?

The intersection where I lived was so brightly lit. I could see the teenagers coming and going, people walking their dogs, and the ever beer-drinking crew of twenty-something dudes who passed through. *I'm so glad to have all that nonsense behind me.* A smile spread across my face.

I switched my music selection to Adele, which was just so soulfully beautiful. As the song "First Love" played, I pictured myself as the little dancer that spins slowly in the jewelry box when it's opened. In my mind, I stood in a beautiful pirouette turning ever so slowly to the tiny pling, pling, pling of the music. When it opened, the soft crack of the velvet came to mind and the music played while I danced to the beautiful melody…round and round.

I couldn't help but think of the love described in the lyrics. The song describes the need to feel alive, to breathe, to feel desire. She is apologizing to her "first love" that she is tired. She needs something new. She is seeking forgiveness. She is through. She wants to taste the kiss from someone new. *Don't we all?* That is the most powerful time. It defies logic and makes no sense at all.

Here's what I know about love. It is the single greatest feeling in the world, felt by all humans, for all humans. It is the universal energy that causes the world to spiral and be in balance at the same time.

I missed it for sure. I missed it on a level of human contact and connection, which made me wonder if I ever knew it at all because I could recall so little about it in my past.

I knew he was out there. I knew he existed. I knew this was in God's perfect timing, and there was nothing I could do to make him feel my love…yet.

There's a plan for love. It's funny how you find yourself in a push-pull with it. You want to pull it into your life even when you know it doesn't feel right. We try to force it so we can feel someone's love. *That's better than no love at all, right?* We know in our gut when a person is not right for us, but the feeling of love – especially new love – is so amazing and so penetrating to our very core. I spent the entire year after my divorce thinking how much I wanted to feel this love, but then later realized that I really needed to love myself first. And yes, it seems very cliché, but you can't give what you don't have for yourself.

The thing is, not everyone fits together. Have you ever looked around and wondered how everyone can be so happy and look and feel so perfect together?

Well, I don't really think every couple is as happy as they appear to be. I'm not saying there is potentially only one soul mate for every person, but the reason they are so hard to find is because not everyone is meant for each other.

It's like searching for a puzzle piece. You have to sort through all the pieces before finding the perfect match. Sometimes you have to go through the entire pile and sometimes it just jumps out at you. This really depends on our ability to receive it…love that is.

And another thing about love, it doesn't just come from the opposite sex. It comes first from God and exists in everything we do, in everything we see, hear and smell. God's love is all around us.

It amazes me how many people feel they cannot be complete without love from a partner. Once we can really love ourselves and accept the love in the universe, we are more prepared to share our life with someone else.

For nearly an hour my eyes bounced back and forth between my computer screen and the falling snow, shining brightly in the intersection. A silhouette emerged from behind the lampposts. Rounding the corner, with his phone to his ear, was Michael. He must have made plans nearby for the evening.

As soon as I recognized him, I smiled. He couldn't see me, but I could see him shuffling his feet in the snow. His cap was shoved down on his head and of course, he was without a coat.

Over the past several months, we had shared many moments together. It was difficult for me to separate intimacy from emotion. My thought is that most people are not capable of it. But I can only speak for myself, from a woman's point of view, and say that it is not possible.

My fondness of Michael grew every day. He was so sweet. I liked him for sure. As our bodies connected, our hearts did too. We would always have a special place for each other.

His lips were so adorably pouty and his brown eyes always looked up at me with a feeling that I'm sure even he couldn't describe.

In the midst of my Michael-consumed thoughts, he looked over at me as if he felt me staring and thinking of him. He looked up and saw me propped up on the counter. Michael put two fingers to his lips and pointed them at me.
I did the same and we just stared at each other for a frozen moment.

Giving up Michael was my New Year's Resolution, it was time. I almost lost him, but we enjoyed each other so much that it was hard to let go for both of us. Being with him had gotten sweeter. We freed our emotions so there were never any expectations. But I wanted to end it so no one got hurt or felt badly when others entered our lives. So yes, it was time to let him go. It was all good. It was exactly the way it should have been.

My conclusion is that Michael came into my life for a reason. He was my friend and we learned from each other. And, who knew, but maybe his feelings ran deeper and I had made a life-long impression on him.

Either way, I kept my heart protected for fear of it being broken. I remained in control of my feelings, but knew I would miss him. I would miss our late night sweetness.

But I would never be far away though. And the day would come when we would have to cross paths, and Michael would have a cute little girlfriend in tow. *How weird that would feel…or maybe even sad?*

But it's not our part to understand why we came together. It was what it was.

So yes, I'm willing to wait for my love, my true love, and no other man will do. He is coming. I believe God sees every lonely moment we have and simply asks us to trust Him. Trust that He will bring it to pass all the desires of our hearts. And so I did.

As the song ended, the pling, pling, pling of the music slowed down and the tiny dancer made a final turn. The red velvet case cracked slowly as it closed down. There was no more music. And then she was asleep. Not long after that, so was I.

At around two in the morning, Michael knocked softly on my door and I let him in. He slid into my warm bed and made love to me until four.

It was love. There was no doubt about it. And though it may not be forever love, it was pretty damn good. Forget those damn resolutions.

Chapter Twenty-Five

Inked…

Head First

After all the thinking and writing about love, the word became a powerful mantra, a powerful belief about life. In line with my quirky, adventurous personality, I took the tiny little "love" doodle scribbled so many times in my journal and made an appointment to get it inked.

I arrived at the tattoo parlor an hour early. *What a nerd!* But I wanted to check the place out to make sure it didn't look shady and full of sleeved creeps. It didn't.

It looked bright and private and all the dudes were funky-looking with piercings and cartoons all over them. They were pretty hot actually, in their own freaky way.

It was all overwhelming though, and my nervousness got the best of me. I walked down to the nearest café to grab a drink, a meal, whatever.

I landed at a cozy, Middle Eastern café. It smelled like foreign food. *Pretty gross.* And the smell drenched my clothes and hair, leaving no traces of the sweet smell of my Coco Mademoiselle.

The music was Mediterranean and all the people who worked there spoke in Arabic. *Why did this always make me feel like they were talking about me?*

The dark red walls and orange lighting made the place feel a little homey. The couches had dark fabric and metallic stitching. A plasma TV sat on the wall and showed exotic dancers. It was a little creepy, but kind of cool.

Anyway, I plopped into the bright orange sofa and made myself comfortable, considering I had an hour to kill.

I was feeling a bit hungry and thought a nice plate of hummus sounded good, but ordered nothing. For a place that smelled entirely of food, the menu consisted entirely of drinks. Nothing but drinks. *Absolute bullshit. How did a full-sized café survive on drinks alone? What the hell?*

I ordered a caramel latte and begged for a muffin, a c-racker or a piece of pita, but got nothing. The waitress brought out what looked like an old piece of baklava. *Isn't baklava Greek?* I'm confused by this ethnic twist, but…gross. *Was this someone's leftovers?* "No thank you." I smiled at the waitress and gave the baklava back. I drank my latte and typed away on my computer.

There was a woman doing some belly dancing across the room. She was a little heavy, not real sexy, but wow, she could really move those hips. *Is this place the Middle Eastern equivalent of a strip club? Hmmm…* I watched her out of the corner of my eye, curiosity growing. How was she moving those hips? She noticed my stare and shimmied over.

"I teach you," she swayed near me.

"Oh…umm…no thank you," I muttered and waived her off. "I'm good." I turned my attention back to the computer screen.

If I wasn't sitting in my full leather coat and scarf, I probably would have gotten up and shook a little like Shakira. *Then again, why the hell not?* Where else can I get a free lesson in belly dancing? I shed my winter paraphernalia and stood at attention for my very first lesson.

It was hilarious. I felt as stiff and crinkly as an unfolded lawn chair. Even after years of yoga, my hips were completely immobile. I did get the hang of it after awhile and started to really enjoy it. My abs got a killer workout.

I shimmied around and looked over my shoulder. A gentleman wandered in and found a seat in a cozy nook by the window.

That was not the weird part. It was what he was doing that was creepier than the anonymous belly dancer. He was smoking what looked like a ginormous bong. It was fancy gold and almost four feet tall sitting on top of the table. It had a long tube that he was puffing away at. *Umm… what the hell? Did I miss something on the menu?* The thing smelled floral and fruity at the same time. *Was he getting some happy smoke? And why was I not partaking in this legal goodness?*

I turned my head and noticed the other employees puffing away across the room. They eyed me up like some kind of woman for purchase. I felt completely out of place with my boring freaking latte. *Damn it…I want to have some happy smoke and more belly dancing.*

If I played my cards right, I just might earn a few bucks along the way with my Shakira-like moves. Have I been living on the wrong side of Chicago long enough to be oblivious to the new ethnic and/or culturally-emerging trends?

"Hi fellas, watchya got there?" I couldn't help myself. I had to know about the pipes. They mumbled and grinned amongst themselves. *Creepy.*

"Hookah, hookah." They said with a smile.

"Hookah, huh? What the hell is that thing?" I said utterly confused.

They went on to explain about the fruit flavored tobacco and laughed at my naiveté. The gentleman smiled at me (again, as if I were for sale).

"Take a drag."

"Whoa...what?" *As if I'm going to just take something from a stranger's mouth and just shove into mine to puff on some anonymous smelling shit.* I could already feel my brother getting ready to kick my ass.

The woman pulled out the menu and showed me all the various Hookah flavors. "It's just like smoking a cigar." *Umm…what the hell?* Curious, I was. And of course there was peer pressure to try this new, hippy, and chic trend.

"Can we swap out the mouthpiece or tip and practice safe smoking?" I asked.

They laughed and handed me a plastic tip for the pipe. It looked like a teeny, tiny plastic condom. I inhaled slowly and could taste apples and other earthly goodness. Then I exhaled slowly. The men laughed. "Oh look at you. You're like a professional!"

"Look at her! She's got it!" The other one chided.

I curtsied and said "Why thank you gentleman." *Note to self: ease up on the cocktail-induced Marlboro Lights.*

It was a bit euphoric, a little wacky and a little relaxing all at the same time.

My new Middle Eastern friends wanted me to stay, but that was just enough yummy Hookah for one night.

I had a date with a needle. It was time to get inked. I made it to my appointment at exactly 7:00 p.m. My artist, Jake, was hot and had nice potential, but he probably had a girlfriend.

We spent an hour fine-tuning the doodle I had prepared for him. The word love, in a beautiful script, that I wanted him to place ever so artistically over my left hip. At the end of the word were two tiny hearts, one for me and one for Joseph.

I waited for him to complete the tracing and observed the artists at work. This place was so cool. The artwork on the walls was all done by the tattoo artists and was bright, controversial, and full of energy. I watched as people had their sleeves worked. Others decided to expand their current tattoos.

The lights were bright fluorescent and behind all the chattering was the hum of the tattoo needles. Bzzzz, bzzzz, bzzzz. All the artists wore latex gloves and had their heads down to focus in on their work.

Jake's tracing on my hip was beautiful. There was no doubt I wanted this ONE word to be the last thing people saw when they shoved my dead ass into a coffin. But seriously though, love is the thing, the only thing. That was it.

Jake had me lay on the table and he got right to work. I was one hundred percent absolutely unprepared for exactly how much pain this was going to be. Sure, I could handle it. *But holy shit. It* REALLY *hurt.*

He pressed and buzzed on my tummy and hip area. I felt a cross between pain and laughter. All I could do for the entire time – about two hours – was hold my breath and try not to cry like a baby. I was actually trying to remember my breathing exercises from my childbirth classes. Three hours later, I didn't care how cute Jake was. I just wanted to get the hell outta there.

The finished product was beautiful and truly stunning. Jake put a large, garbage bag-like bandage over it. Motrin was definitely in order. All I could think about was my bed. I had plans to meet Michael later, but there was no way in hell that was going to happen. My entire side was swollen and sore.

When I made it home I collapsed, garbage bag and all. It took a few weeks to heal, but I couldn't wait to show that baby off. After attending my Bikram Yoga class only days later, it looked like it was all going to melt off with the sweat. But slowly, the love tattoo healed and looked beautiful.

When I showed Joseph, he looked at it with the biggest eyes and said, "Mom, you are so cool. I am REALLY happy for you." *Huh…who would have thought my little guy would love it as much as I did?* But then again, he is his mother's son.

Chapter Twenty-Six

That One Percent...

Head First

Ninety-nine percent of the time I had my head on straight. I was in control of my emotions and knew just what the hell I was doing.

The other one percent really sucked. I used to wonder why so many single people I knew had cereal for dinner. Now, I understand. At times, it's merely a matter of economics, but at other times, it's basically, "why bother?"

As a single mom, I couldn't help but let thought monsters creep in occasionally. If I weren't human, this would be impossible. But I am. So from time-to-time, my armor slips off and I get all caught up in the bullshit.

Right after the new year, I came up with a new plan. I decided to forgo random dating and just focus on my work and my writing, and to break up with Michael every other week.

But I was still seeing Michael because I was incapable of keeping a single New Year's resolution. And really, what was the point of giving him up?

I was confident that my plan, though slightly dysfunctional, compared to my married friends' standards, was a good one. And the thing was I didn't really give a shit what people thought. I did what I did when I wanted to do it and no one could stand in judgment of me.

It was a brilliant way to live. With that said, I found a curious level of stress creeping into my work environment. As my star began to rise even higher, I found there were several people around me who wanted to lasso my bright glow and keep me from doing my shining thing.

I was not having this. I would not tolerate little people who felt threatened by my fabulousness to ruin my life. But damn it, they tried.

The stress grew daily. It seeped into the water coolers – in the bathrooms – and everywhere I went. The stress started to affect me. And I didn't like my work anymore. I loved working with amazing people but each day felt like a noose hung around my neck.

For the first time in my corporate career, I wondered how I would survive without my paycheck. I dreamed about this and woke in the middle of the night panicked about how I would live without my healthy six-figure salary.

I didn't want to quit. I didn't even want to change companies, much less careers, at this point in my life. But life was too short to live with this stress.

I started to not like the mother and friend I was becoming. I was short with my son. I was short with my friends, even when I did take the time to talk to them.

This went on for a few months before I faced the bullshit of it all. This was not good.

On top of that, the pressure mounted. My lease was up in two months and I was still no closer to finding a home than I was six months ago when I started looking.

Additionally, my commission checks were not coming. The financial pressure hit me during a stroll through BCBG. I could easily drop a grand in forty-five minutes. This was ridiculous.

I was almost forty and changing careers was not part of my plan. I remembered sitting at my desk one day and staring at my computer while another crisis unfolded. The droning ring of the cell phone blared in my head and the voicemails mounted by the minute.

It was time to step away from this situation to see clearly. I called my friend Ann and cried into the phone.

"What's the difference between ordinary and extraordinary?" She interrupted my tears.

"Extra?" I hesitated, not sure of what she was getting at.

"Yes, but YOU are extraordinary and you're forgetting that," she paused. "Don't let this situation define you. You're better than that. My friend never quits." That was all my ears needed to hear.

I pulled away from my desk, shut the computer off and put the phone in the refrigerator (I'm still unclear about this one. Unfortunately, it didn't kill the phone).

I went to Bikram. You know, when the world kicks your ass, Bikram Yoga will always be there, like a loving mistress. She will put you among a bunch of half-naked people, turn up the heat to 105 degrees, and twist and contort you in ways that will make you forget whatever it was that was on your mind.

On the way home, I stopped at the fire house where my brother worked. I wanted to feel a big brother hug and most of all, his love. The firemen on his shift all knew me and greeted me with smiles and hugs. When I walked in, I felt like part of his family there. Milt, one of my favorite men on the job, greeted me especially warm. He was the cook and he always fed me after yoga. Each time I arrived there in my shower-wet clothes and matted down hair, he always sat and ate with me. We chatted about all kinds of things. Being there was always like being at home.

"Giaaaaaaa! Hey kid where you been?" Milt greeted me.

"Hi honey…I've been around, just doing my thang!"

"Pull up a chair. I'm serving your favorite – ribs." Milt did make a fabulous batch of ribs, and I always brought an appetite with me.

Being there made me so proud. My brother was so well respected by these men, they loved each other like brothers, and then there was me, "Joe's sister."

I blasted the radio on the way home and danced like the car was my stage. My favorite songs of the moment played and helped me feel right: *Right and Round* by Flo Rida and *Dead and Gone* by T.I.

But of course, nothing got this girl going like a little *Sexbomb* by Tom Jones. It worked though. A little music and a little dancing always worked. It reminded me of who I am, crazy and free.

It released my tension and with the kind of weeks I'd been having at work, I needed to let it go for fear I'd end up on WGN's breaking news, "Stressed employee walks into work dressed up like the Joker." *Yes, I am capable. Yes, it was that bad.*

It has been my habit to spend at least twenty minutes each night in meditation. As a firm believer that the screenplay running in my mind would be the actual film of my life, it is important to keep the actors in check, and of course, modifying the lines and images where needed. And I can't lie to you, this time alone is an incredibly important part of my life.

If you actually sit in stillness, then you can hear the answers to your questions. You can find the direction, the advice, and the connection between the dots in your life.

So I sat in meditation until my knees and feet were basically numb. With each breath I inhaled and believed courage was in and fear was out. I breathed love in and hatred out. I nestled into my chocolate brown Egyptian cotton sheets, LDM at my side and looked up, not at anything in particular, just toward heaven where my Dad was always close.

I smiled because it reminded me of all the other shit I'd been through over the past years. Nothing gets me down. I am never out of the fight.

Thoughts of the past year crept into my mind. All the tears shed by my son and I over the divorce. Vivid memories of sitting Joseph down at the edge of the bed and explaining to him that "shit happens" and it's not what happens to you, it's what you do about it. So accept it and deal with it. I remember Joseph's big brown eyes looking up at me and smiling through his tears. He hugged me so tightly that day. That moment confirmed that God brought Joseph and I together for a reason. We needed each other in this life. This was all part of the plan.

Soon after revisiting my memories, I drifted off to sleep. It turned out to be the most perfect night. Around three in the morning, my slumber was disturbed by a loving familiar feeling. It was my dad. I prayed for him to be near. I wanted to feel him again just like I did so many times in the past.

His warm energy washed over me. He told me not to worry. That once again, I was going to be alright.

The energy was like a warm embrace. My cares drifted away as I sunk deeper into my bed. It felt like I was floating, almost soaring. It was a beautiful feeling.

I awoke to the beeping of my phone at nine. A text from Michael, "Where are you this beautiful Saturday morning and when can I see you again?"

"When fate will allow it," I texted him back.

I was through trying to engineer my own life. I was done trying to put a stronghold on situations until they worked out the way I believed they should.

I was attached to an outcome here that was causing me stress because I saw no other way. With my trust in God, I finally released the wheel. *Ah… peace.*

Saturday morning was beautiful. The sun was shining, the sky was blue. At any rate this was the type of Saturday morning that a year earlier, I would have found myself dragging out of bed without any sense of life, drowning in self-pity. The sounds of Saturday morning were different now. It used to start with my son running into bed with me, snuggling, tickling and playing, mixed with the smell of bacon and coffee traveling through the house. And, to top it off, the annoying laughter of SpongeBob in the background.

It took a long time to accept that Saturday now looked different. Saturday had a whole new feel, smell, and look. Now there was almost no sound to Saturday when I woke up. There were no smells. My LDM and I still look around for Joseph, but the reality of the situation is that this is my life. THIS was my choice and I could either become unglued and waste it in tears, or I could wake up, light my favorite vanilla candles, crank up the music and do WHATEVER THE HELL I WANTED!

I was no longer attached to the fact that Saturday had to look a certain way. I could change it up WHENEVER I wanted and that was the only way to look at this.

In just twelve hours, my mood transitioned from shitty to amazing. *Tell me, how powerful is the mind?*

I saddled up once again, third day in a row of Bikram Yoga; sadistic, yet fabulous. Only this time, I stopped at Stuart Weitzman on the way back. I'm only human.

Chapter Twenty-Seven

Sweet & Crazy...

Love

I wish I could pretend he meant nothing to me, that we were intimate, and nothing more.

It was weird because he was so much younger, but when we were together it felt so sweet. The reality was that we would never have a real relationship. But Michael and I had something special that was undeniably good.

We both had our separate lives. When I wasn't out doing my own crazy things, and when he wasn't out trying to make his mark in the world, we would find ourselves together. As time grew, it felt sweet and comfortable.

It was a crisp Spring night, like most April nights in Chicago. Winter lingered and the air was still cold. I was out with friends having an amazing time, dancing my ass off at Sub 51 after a delicious sushi meal at Sushisamba Rio's on Wells Street.

I wore a beautiful black dress with white and grey stripes. It fit almost like a tube top that hugged my thighs. Tights and black patent leather stilettos accompanied my feet. And a tiny black leather jacket completed the outfit, and it was beautiful for a night out on the town.

Michael was in town, but he was out with friends. I respected his time with the guys. I didn't expect to see him and I was okay with it.

There were many male takers this evening and plenty of good times all around. Between the dudes with the bad pick-up lines and cheesy Aqua Di Gio cologne, these guys just weren't my style. But it always made for an amusing evening.

After our rounds of drinks, dancing, and lots of laughter, my friends dropped me off in front of my house around three that morning. I felt pretty tired coming down from the music and good times.

I ripped off my dress and couldn't wait to take my makeup off and crawl into bed. It was handy to have such stamina from all the yoga, but shit, I was worn out. Perhaps my days of staying out 'til the early dawn, were coming to an end. That really wouldn't be a bad thing.

But my phone kept beeping with text messages. "Hey sexy, where you at?" his text read.

"Home in bed…alone."

"Where were you tonight?" He asked.

I was tired and didn't have time for small talk. I left the door unlocked for him. His car pulled up in twenty minutes flat. When he entered the house, I wore a big smile. He looked older for some reason. *Had we really been together that long?*

His hair and eyes were dark. He had a shadow of stubble on his face and his lips were pouty and full. I gasped when I saw him. He looked so good. He was not even on the last step in my home. We leapt for each other and started kissing.

We touched and stared at each other. Chemistry is so beautiful. We didn't have to have an ending or an outcome. All we needed was the moment.

Moments like this were so amazing. They came from someplace real and wonderful. They light you up and make you feel alive. This was one of those moments. Michael and I had something very sweet and nothing could ever make me forget the times we had together.

We kissed and pulled each other close. We pushed each other around the walls and across the room to my bed. He threw me down hard and pressed his lips on me like we would never see each other again.

I knew his kiss. I knew his look. I knew his body. I knew the soft shadow of his face in the darkness. Time will do that.

Michael made love to me that night and it was better than it had ever been. We touched for hours and then grew tired and ready for sleep. He plopped himself up on my bed and sat up on his elbows. His big brown eyes looked sleepily at me. The lamp was dim and the smelled of vanilla candle permeated the air.

Michael dropped his head on the pillow and his hand stroked my shoulder gently. We talked for almost an hour and in that beautiful moment one would never know there was more than ten years between us. He was adorable. We were adorable.

Michael didn't want to leave. And I didn't want him to go. But the reality of our relationship hitting daylight was unrealistic because of our age difference. He was only twenty-six and carried a full class load, working towards his MBA. But we had these special times.

Sometimes in life you just take what you can get and love the ride. I loved the ride and I wouldn't trade those moments for anything. But I knew it was time to let him go. My body could not stay separate from my heart and eventually, I would want more from him than he could ever give me. But I just couldn't let go.

We were so comfortable with each other. We knew each other well and when we were together, nothing else mattered.

Our feelings were obvious and it was honest. Yet still, he couldn't be the man I needed or wanted him to be. It just was not possible.

One thing I knew for sure was that when it ended, it was going to hurt. That was easy to predict.

Even though I had been down this road a million times before, I knew what I knew all those other times. Life is too short and you take moments of wonderful when they come to you. You can't live in fear of being hurt. You have to jump in and take chances. My jumping in with Michael was worth every minute. So I decided to give him up when I was ready to give him up, and not a minute sooner.

Chapter Twenty-Eight

He was Not there...

Love

Head First

It was May again. And just like many other years, Dad came to my memory. It was 13 years to the day of his death.

This time around my heart was heavy. My life was amazing and I couldn't have asked for more, but nothing could replace what was lost. There would always be that special place that held memories of my dad.

I hadn't driven past my childhood home in about 10 years and for some reason it was calling me. My mother moved out several years earlier and there was just no reason to go back. But on this day, the time had come. I was being drawn there and needed to say goodbye. I wasn't living in Chicago when my mother moved out, so I felt compelled to go back and see the house.

I traveled through the city with a great flood of memories at every corner. Twenty-three years of my life were spent here. There were very few streets I hadn't driven down, restaurants I hadn't eaten at, or places where I hadn't made a friend or two.

Turning onto the street almost made me feel sick. There were great memories there; sad ones and happy ones, along with all the history. No matter how the neighborhood may have changed, they would always live on this street.

Some of the homes had become quite dilapidated and others looked almost exactly the same. I rounded the corner and my old home came into view. Tears poured down my face. Honoring Dad's life and his death was important to me. I had forgotten how tiny the house was, how uneventful, yet comfortable. The cracks in the pavement hadn't changed and the old tree stump still remained in the yard as a reminder that our tree once stood tall there. Nothing seemed to have changed. Even the front door and the blinds on the window were the same. It all still looked just as it was.

The landscaping barely changed. It felt like any other Sunday afternoon visit to my parents' house. Mom was famous for her cooking. Sunday was her day and she loved when her children were home.

After dinner, we usually sat outside together. We could see what was going on in the whole neighborhood because the house next to ours had been taken down and the lot was empty and large. Dad spent a lot of time out here. He'd have friends over and they'd drink beer and play cards while my brother and I came and went.

Later in his years, there were fewer people that came by. Then it was mostly just Mom and Dad.

I can remember so many times, sitting outside with my dad and watching people pass by on the street. Most of my memories are of Dad in his wheelchair. He always sat outside just to take in the beauty of the outdoors and things around him. He always seemed so content being surrounded by nature.

The addition he built in the back of the house seemed more impressive now than it did at the time when I was forced to help hang drywall and lay flooring. Dad used to make me do work that I absolutely hated all the time. I smiled through my tears, just remembering our handiwork together.

In his earlier years, Dad always walked around with his white cotton T-shirt and his tool belt that hung too low on his waist. He'd be sweating bullets under the hot Chicago sun and build away with his pencil tucked straight behind his ear.

The music of Dean Martin was always heard when Dad was around. He'd sing to the tunes while climbing up and down the ladder.

All these moments went unappreciated when I was younger, but now I see them with complete adoration. I can still hear him singing, "…standing on the corner…watching all the girls go by…."

Dad's favorite and most often asked question of my brother and I was, "Hey kid, what's the greatest room in the world?"

"What Dad?" we'd ask.

"Room for improvement," he'd always answer. He got us with that one every time.

Dad wasn't perfect though. His life was no monument to fatherhood. There were many difficult years, especially when it came to his constant battle with alcohol. But in the end, you can't change the past. I can't fault him. I can only forgive.

There were plenty of times I turned to my brother to be the man in my life, my father figure.

But I still was always Dad's little girl. He loved me with everything he had. This I knew for sure. Dad was part of my plan. He was chosen to be my father long before I was put on this earth. He was part of who I am today. I never want to change that.

I parked my car in front of the house and hoped no one would think of me as a stalker. This was something I needed to take in. It was amazing to see how little the new owners had changed things. The address fixtures were the same, only the six had fallen off. The large pots for flowers my mother used to adorn with geraniums were empty and had only weeds coming through.

The window of my parents' room beckoned me. Thirteen years ago, the gust of wind came in and carried my dad's soul away. The memory will forever remain etched in my heart. In spite of Dad's death, there were many great memories here.

Not every memory here is about his death and it would be a dishonor to my mother not to acknowledge how she raised us. How she brought us together as a family for holidays. How she cooked Sunday suppers (and Monday through Saturday too). The smell of her chicken soup warmed our little house and she made a good life for us.

Glancing at the front yard, I remembered playing ball with my brother. I laughed just thinking about how one winter we played army and he broke my collarbone while pummeling me into the snow. And then I remembered the times I crawled onto the roof for ultimate tanning. And I'll never forget when I first learned to ride my bike.

One home, so many things. It all happened here. Slowly my car eased away. There was no need for me to return. I took some pictures for my memories. I was thankful for my upbringing there because it made me who I am today. It was all part of the plan for my life. It was all the way it was supposed to be. I wouldn't trade it for anything.

But the memories of my dad don't end here. There was one more stop to make to honor his life. I had flowers to take to the cemetery, including a single blue carnation. The same as the one I wore on the day of Dad's funeral. It was the color of his eyes and the color of my eyes.

That day was rainy and chilly, the perfect cliché to a cemetery visit. My tires crunched over the gravel of the cemetery road while I searched for the Sassafras tree. I parked close to what I thought was Dad's plot. But walking over with my heels sticking to the moist soil, I realized I was nowhere close. For a moment, panic struck me. *Had the grass grown over the headstone?*

Then at last, with my patent leather stilettos covered in mud and the hems of my pants wet and soiled, I found Dad. My tears fell sooner than I'd expected. The flowers my mother left were there. She still came after all these years to honor his memory.

I placed my carnation in the flower vase and knelt at his grave. But I knew he wasn't there. His words surrounded me. "I'm not there…I'm not there."

And he wasn't. He was in my heart and that would never change. There was something so powerful about remembering the place we laid his body to rest. The beautiful blue satin in his coffin that I so carefully chose was six feet under. His rosary was still there, along with pictures of the family. My brother's old football jersey was also there. But Dad was not.

My feet were frozen and my eyes focused on Dad's headstone. His arms covered me. His love and support would always be with me. There were so many times I called for him just to feel his sweet embrace over the past few years. He never failed me, he always came to me when I called on him. Tears clung to my cheeks and dropped with big splashes onto his headstone.

Dad was a motor machinist in the U.S. Navy. To this day, I still don't really understand what that was, but I knew that at the age of fifteen, Dad was in World War II. Most people in this world would never live a life like his. By eighteen he had seen and done more than most ever will in a lifetime.

To rest Dad, to rest. That's what they say when people die, that they went to rest. All I know is he was taken too early, but God wrote his plan for everyone. This happened to be Dad's.

On his death bed, Dad asked me what I thought Heaven was like. Back then, at 26, my answer was very different than it is now. Now, I believe Heaven is peace, just peace. There are no outlines, borders, or shapes in Heaven. Just peace, soaring and loving peace. And I believed my father was at peace. He was not merely sleeping six feet below me. He was at peace.

Chapter Twenty-Nine

Reflections Part Deux...

Love

You can divorce yourself from your spouse, or the life you had, but you can't erase the time, the moments or the things that remain unchanged. *And really, why would you want to?*

Once I realized my marriage was over, I decided that having another baby would solve everything. Sometimes you hold on to a dream any way you can. You believe the dream is worth any sacrifice and you do anything to keep it alive.

Unfortunately for us, getting pregnant had become a full-time job. In fact, after three rounds of IVF, back-to-back, I realized not only were we out $40,000, but it felt like a tremendous sign. A very expensive, painful sign.

There comes a time in every woman's life where she comes face-to-face with two things: the spongy, absorbent tip of a pregnancy test and the bottom of the toilet bowl. This can occur many times in her life and begin at any age.

In our early days, we pee on sticks and hold our breath, hoping and waiting that nothing will show in the little circle. And each time we sit on the toilet, we wait anxiously for the red to drop so the month can begin anew.

The story changes as we get older. This time we pee on an outrageous amount of sticks before our period's due date, with bated breath, the results will be positive. In this case, we also develop a similar anxiety when sitting on the pot. But this time, we are hoping that NO red will drop to the bottom of the bowl. We don't want the month to begin anew. I was no different during the waiting time between my procedure and the HCG test. Those were two weeks of absolute hell.

I tried to remain positive and I tried to slip into my normal groove of thinking the time would pass. NOT. Sure, time would tick by, but not without traces of my neurosis. Each time I went to the bathroom, I thought for sure the red would drop and it would be all over.

In the middle of a sentence, I'd run into the bathroom because I was sure my period was coming. This was insane. Even while driving down the road, I'd feel sure I had my period and race to the nearest bathroom to check.

It was humorous to think of this now, but there was something so unnatural about this process that made me crazy. Not to mention the mood swings, combined with my inability to cope with this long timeframe of uncertainty. My first round of IVF was a failure. Period, literally.

Three days before my first HCG test of my second round, I decided to self-protect. I became committed to the notion that this second time did NOT work and my period would come in a few days. So I automatically became bitchy and disappointed so that when Monday came and the nurse called with that soft, comforting voice to confirm my negative HCG, I'd be prepared.

I was impossible to live with. Joseph, who was five years old at the time, was cautious around me. "Excuse me honey, Mommy's a little nuts right now. So, could you please just give me a little space?"

One Sunday I decided to buy a pregnancy test, the sworn enemy of my twenties. The nurses at the reproductive clinic had been adamant that I NOT pee on any stick because it would likely create a false negative result. *Blah, blah, blah. I had to know.*

I waited for the first morning urine. I followed the instructions on the box even though I barely slept the night before because of the anticipation. But it was also because my backside was covered in lumps from the nightly progesterone shots. Bruises covered both my cheeks.

At six that morning, I shot up like a kid at Christmas. Without even putting on my glasses or brushing my teeth, I ran downstairs and opened my little package in secrecy. I wrestled with the plastic covering on the box, all while my heart pounded and my hands trembled.

Again, pure insanity overtook me. I peed on the stick and watched immediately for the vertical line to cross the horizontal. Much to my self-protected mode, the vertical line appeared…the test was positive.

The stick was covered in pee. I made sure to give it the full seven seconds and, well, I had to pee pretty badly. I stared at the stick for minutes. I checked and rechecked the instructions to make sure I read them correctly. I ran towards the stairs to tell my husband, but decided to recheck the instructions one more time.

Positive was positive and that was good enough for me. My feet glided up the stairs. "I just peed on a stick and it's positive!" My husband woke from his slumber and looked at me through fuzzy eyes.

He cocked his head and said, "That's good, right?" *Oh, Lord, help me. I'll give him that one for being tired.*

I dressed and headed to my HCG blood draw, which they insisted needed to be done by seven in the morning. I drove in silent prayer. Everything in the world was starting new that day. And I WAS PREGNANT.

My husband called my cell and chatted about what room we'd put the baby in, how we could tell our son, etc., etc. He was so excited and fully absorbed the positive news.

I waited in the line for my blood draw and wanted to shout my news to the world, but decided better of it considering the variety of places the other ladies might be in their cycle and/or success. This was my secret and I wasn't going to fear the call this time. I'd embrace it and celebrate it.

When the nurse called later that day to confirm my results, she sang, *Happy Birthday* since the embryo transfer had been done on my birthday.

"Happy Birthday Mom…and congratulations you're pregnant!" she exclaimed.

"I know, I know, I know. I peed on the stick," I confessed. She quickly scolded me, but then we giggled together. She confirmed my HCG had gone to 57, just where she wanted it to be. *Wooo hooo. I was on my way.*

"Come back in two days so we can verify that the HCG will double."

"Yes Ma'am!" I shared my good news with my girlfriends who had supported me through the endless days of self-protecting, questioning, and all the emotions one goes through during this process. I saved all the messages on my cell that celebrated our good news.

Two days later, I reported back to the blood draw station still elated and feeling special. I had succeeded in getting pregnant, a task physicians assured me was very difficult, given the history of our ability to get pregnant in this marriage. I guess I fooled them.

My husband developed a look on his face that always greeted me with, "How are you feeling?" Or, he'd greet me on the phone by saying, "Hey, little Momma."

I sat in the draw chair that was separated from other patients by a small partition. It completely lacked privacy, but it was just a blood draw. The girl next to me talked animatedly about her HCG done on Monday that was 400.

"Four hundred," she said through the partition. "Can you believe that? I must have three or four in there." The phlebotomists congratulated her and chatted amongst each other about how awesome that was, and blah, blah, blah. *Who the hell does this bitch think she is with her four hundred?*

The four hundred bitch, of course was not really a bitch. How would I know that? But she was extremely insensitive to the other ten or so women who hovered in the halls. I mean, so what she was 400? Did she have to go bragging to the entire facility? I felt like such an underachiever with my little old 57. *Was that even accurate? Are they even sure I was pregnant? Four hundred?* That bothered me all day.

For some reason, I worried all day about getting the call from the nurse. I was anxious and then started to question just when in the hell I could actually take a breath and relax a little.

I was in a meeting at work when my cell rang. "Excuse me everyone." I stepped out for the call. Immediately, I recognized the tone of the nurse's voice. *Why in the hell would she be taking that sad, serious tone?*

"Gia, the HCG didn't double – not even close," she said. "We are very concerned. There is a 50 percent chance these numbers will climb and all could be well."

"But there is the other 50 percent, right?" I asked sadly. *Here we go again.*

"Yes, you're right," she tried to reassure me. "We've got to wait two more days to find out if you're pregnant."

I was certain this whole process was going to kill me. If not, I would surely do it myself by inducing a massive heart attack.

I never returned to my meeting, but had another one later that day that was extremely important. I called my husband, my friends and my doctor friends. I had to gather some girlfriend statistics and more knowledge about HCG.

Throughout the course of the afternoon, I gained enough info to feel that the scenario was not hopeless, but false hope would be futile at this point.

I was absolutely tired. I kept playing wait and see with my HCG and the outcome just did NOT feel positive. I cried for the next hour and tried to understand how this happened. How could I come to peace with the probable outcome?

I wondered with bitter jealousy, what the results were for the 400 bitch. I saw her the next day for our equally timed blood draws. We both arrived early and stood outside the door in the cool September morning. I pulled my baseball cap down low to avoid eye contact with her. *Why couldn't the doors open already so I could get this over with?*

I stood there and admired my painted toe nails. They actually looked pretty good in the deep burgundy color. I kept my gaze low as I was not in the mood to share my story. Then suddenly, the 400 bitch spoke to me.

"Hello," I said. I couldn't avoid being polite.

"I remember you from the other day. I'm here having my HCG drawn again."

"Okay." I said.

"My first draw was 400 and my second was over 800." I couldn't miss the excitement in her voice. I shoved my hands deeper into my pockets.

AGAIN…*with the 400? Is that all this lady can talk about? Are we supposed to stop by her gift registry for her quads on the way home?* I was so fed up with this woman whose name I didn't even know. She was going on and on.

"You know, the doctors diagnosed me with early menopause when I was 37." She explained to us. "I've been using donor eggs for the past three years. I've thawed the last three and only two progressed, so I had to transfer two, and now, one or both of them have doubled." So that was it. That was her story.

I, of course, felt a wave of remorse for having called her the 400 bitch, but who could blame me? I guess she had her cross to bear and she deserved her good fortune, though many would debate that multiples create obvious health risks. But I doubt that really crossed her mind at this point.

I guess I made peace with her that day, thinking maybe I was just so pissed off about my own numbers. And when in the hell did we start measuring all of the numbers? I know many women who wouldn't even know they are getting an HCG test when they report to their doctor for the first prenatal visit. This was a very insane process and the emotional roller coaster was both exhausting and unnatural.

So I waited for the results. AGAIN. I had talked to several people and they were all pulling for me. My doctor friends convinced me to have hope and to not despair.

When I laid my head on the pillow, I was even too tired to talk to God. I closed my eyes and left messages for Him and hoped He'd check them.

My hope was that the numbers would climb and the HCG would be normal, or they would drop, my period would start and I could begin to put this behind me. What I prayed did NOT happen.

The nurse called and said the numbers climbed a little, to 87, but I had to retest in two more days. Well, at this point, I was so tired I couldn't even cry or believe the turn of events over the course of five days. Pregnant on Monday. Not pregnant the next Monday.

So over the weekend, I not only self-protected again, but I waited for the red to drop. This time, I hoped it would do so soon so I could just get on with my life. I didn't call my friends, doctors or any others. I didn't want to feel pity or despair.

I went in for what I hoped was my final blood draw. I was in no hurry to get this blood draw done. I did not arrive early at the lab, nor did I really care what was going on with the other ladies. I did, however, feel like telling all the others that they shouldn't get excited about a positive pregnancy test. There was NO time to relax in this process. Plus, it really sucks to spend $15,000 and have absolutely nothing to show for it, but a broken heart and a bruised ass. But because I was not the uncaring, insensitive person I was in my head, I said nothing.

Later that day, I saw the familiar number come through on my cell phone. "How low is it?" I asked the nurse.

"The numbers have actually gone down, Gia." She said with compassion in her voice. "We need to have you stop your meds and wait for a period. I'm so sorry for this. You know how much I really wanted this for you."

"Thanks." I hung up the phone. I sobbed in my husband's arms for what seemed like hours. I saw it coming and tried to protect myself. But in the end I still felt like shit and couldn't muster up the courage or strength to do anything but cry.

Later that night, I woke up to the twinge of pain I'd known for years. When I sat on the toilet, there it was.

The red dropped, and it dropped AGAIN after round three. No more.

Chapter Thirty

Girl, Glue, My Rock...

Head First

I sat on the couch, watched her and smiled. I met this girl eight years ago and fell in love with her the minute I met her. She was tall, gorgeous and Mediterranean, a real Greek beauty. Her big brown eyes were the most remarkable I had ever seen.

And there was something about her voice and the way she articulated her words with her hands. She always made me stop and listen as if nothing else mattered in the world.

Zoe was my rock. She taught me how to talk to God. She taught me to have faith. Zoe was there for me every day of my life before, during, and after my divorce. She always listened, never judged and just held me each time I cried.

On the day of my divorce trial, she flew in to be at my side. When her tall, beautiful frame came up the stairs, I knew everything was going to be alright. Her strength was ever-present. She sat on the old wooden bench outside the courtroom and squeezed my hand tight. She was among what I like to call my "Glue Girl" that day, including Mom, Ashley, and of course, AJ.

You can never repay love like that. You can just know that God surrounds us with angels.

Sipping my hazelnut coffee and watching her play with her children on the floor, I began remembering the day she phoned me about her pregnancy with Alex. It was her third and very unexpected baby. I was in the grocery store and heard the strain in her voice when she called. "Girl, there's something I have to tell you, it's my health," she said. "But I don't want to talk about it right now." I couldn't see straight, the tears rushed to my eyes and blocked my vision. I thought she was going to tell me she had breast cancer or something tragic.

"What?" I said and pulled my cart over. I started balling. Zoe stopped me and said, "No, no, wait. I'm pregnant."

"Excuse me?" I could have killed her. I could have reached through the phone and slapped the shit out of her. My tears turned to joy and instant relief. But still, I could have killed her.

Alex was now one and Zoe was such a beautiful mother. She was a woman of great faith. She had been through so much in her life. She had been through things that would make others crack and crumble, but not Zoe, not my girl.

Zoe taught everyone around her about God. She never started a meal without a prayer. She never let a Sunday pass without taking her family to praise God. I envied that about her. I didn't have that kind of discipline.

One Sunday, Joseph and I went to church with her. On the way there, we listened to the song, *Word of God Speak*. All the kids sang. The song was such a beautiful song about being at God's mercy; no words, just needing and listening. The church we went to was packed and it was a little intimidating for me. I'd only been to a Catholic church for the past thirty-something years. There were no organs or fancy robes here, just people coming together to worship God. At one point in the celebration they asked people with special requests to come forward and kneel together. Zoe whisked me up there with her and her husband. I knelt down between them, bowed my head and shut my eyes tight. I was overwhelmed with tears.

I had a lot of special requests, apparently. I wanted so much pain to go away and I wanted answers. Worry consumed my mind. Zoe and her husband Mark squeezed my hands tight.

There was so much love here. God's arms were around us. I was in a different place. I experienced such a great feeling of love and surrender that when I pulled myself up, I felt both exhausted and exhilarated at the same time. I left all my worries there that day.

I gave them all to God, and for once…just once, I could be free. Zoe taught me that. She was my rock. When trouble found me, I called her and she gave me that gift every single time.

We'd been friends for years and nothing changed that. Years may have passed but my girl was still the same. She loved her lime green and hot pink things. She put feta cheese on just about everything. She painted her toes with the same polish, *It's all Greek to Me*, from OPI. She always had a cool hand bag. Zoe accessorized even when going to get groceries, and she always, always, made me feel more at home in her arms than anyone else in the world.

When Joseph and I drove home from the airport after our visit with Zoe, I played the CD she made us. When the song, *Word of God Speak* came on, Joseph's voice remained soft while he sang.

Then his words disappeared into the darkness. His sniffles filled the air. I almost ran the car off the road, while my head turned around to see what was wrong.

I flipped the light on and saw him sitting there with his big brown eyes filled with tears. They ran slowly down his cheeks. His chin quivered and he looked overwhelmed.

"Joseph, baby, what's wrong?" He sat in silence.

"Please tell Mom what's wrong."

"Nothing Mom," Joseph replied. "This song is just so beautiful, it makes me cry."

At that moment, I cried with him. I cried at that moment. I cried *for* that moment. He squeezed my hand tight and I knew this time would be etched in my heart forever. My Rock had touched another heart of mine.

She may never know how many times I thanked God for her. She may never know how deeply my love goes for her.

Together, we had our moments: pedicures and shopping, raising our children together, our trips to NYC that ended at five in the morning at the McDonald's on Broadway, standing strong. We were always together and side-by-side when we needed each other. I knew without a doubt we would grow old together. We would at every age, be sharing our stories and our love.

Chapter Thirty-One

Cougars and MILFs...

Head First

I resent the term *Cougar*. Every time I hear it, I cringe. The image that comes to mind is one of an older woman; powerful and wealthy who is nulliparous, and bored with her life cause she gave it all up for her beloved career which has now left her feeling empty and alone. She's got cash, and she gets after the boys. No thanks.

Many a man has tried to change my image of this *Cougar*, but to no avail.

MILF is another term that makes me uneasy. I get it, the acronym, Mother I'd Like to F---. Technically it could be considered flattering. But to me, it implies that a woman's sexuality is broken down into categories based on whether or not she had children.

That said, as a single and fabulous gal, I can see the attraction to younger men. They're less self-absorbed, they're high energy, and they are more fun than stuffy corporate jockeys.

But here's the thing: I NEVER went looking for younger men. They found me. They always found me. It was almost like clockwork at a bar, or anywhere.

I find myself spending time with many a backward hat-wearing chap talking about absolutely nothing, feeling absolutely no responsibility or weird competition.

I do enjoy meeting people of all ages, and truthfully, since my divorce, I have dated men from 22 to 53. It's all good experience. Every age offers something different and amazing. From Vegas to Mexico, and back to Chicago it was all good. I enjoyed having a great time taking care of ME, figuring out who I am and what I want to do with my life. Though I'm reluctant to date anyone seriously, I am fascinated with my options.

What I can't figure out is why my twenty-something single girlfriends were dating men my age and the men my age were scared to death of women like me.

I took a trip with my son to the Riviera Maya in June after my divorce the previous November. This decision was made on a boring Tuesday when I felt I needed to get away. So I booked the trip and four days later we were off.

The resort was Italian owned, so it was chock full of Europeans. This only meant that they were difficult to understand, and it left me explaining why men swam in what looked like underwear to my son.

On our third day in, we were tan and happy and enjoying everything the world could offer.

After a long day on a snorkeling excursion, we found ourselves once again at the pool shortly after dusk. While Joseph and I played in the pool, he had me atop his shoulders in the fireman's carry. I looked up and noticed a very attractive Italian gentleman staring down at me.

There was a bar overlooking the pool with giant windows that people could literally sit on and stare out over the pool. He sat on the window ledge and his legs dangled over. His eyes were dark and piercing. He had jet black hair that was wavy and his stare was intense. He had the fullest lips and his tan was dark. As the night grew darker, the whites of his eyes glowed from the balcony. His stares were borderline uncomfortable.

After what seemed like forever, he came down with his friends into the pool and offered up a game of pool volleyball. Joseph and I obliged.

We did a formal introduction. His name was Salvador. His English was terrible and my Italian was minimal at best. It was like a Tarzan and Jane introduction.

"Me, Salvador."

"Me, Gia," I responded back. We smiled.

But Joseph was on to this guy. He watched over me like a hawk. It was actually the first time a man had been so assertive with me in front of him.

We played volleyball as the sun set and the pool grew empty. The DJ played Biggie Smalls, *Big Poppa*, in the background.

Salvador dove and played around me. My son was amused at the attention he showed me.

"Are you married?" Salvador asked me.

"No, she's divorced and we're in room 2130." Joseph responded before I could utter a word. I shot Joseph a stare that told him how inappropriate it was to give our number out like that. He looked up at me shy and apologetic.

Salvador continued to stare me down. His volleyball was terrible and he flirted like crazy. When the volleyball game was over, we sat at the side of the pool while my son swam with some kids. We really didn't understand each other. I came to understand his age was 28 and he didn't even ask my age.

"You go to dance with me tonight?" He asked.

"Umm…noooo," I said with a grin and pointed to Joseph.

"Bella," he said. "Molto bella," meaning very beautiful.

"Grazie," I said, remembering the CD on how to speak Italian that I'd started listening to earlier in the year.

Salvador had an intense stare and his eyes were like huge almonds, but very, very dark. His hair and skin were dark too, which made his wavy black hair and curls dance around his eyes.

There was no doubt he was beautiful. He was typically Italian in that he was dark, romantic and flirty. He was very clear about wanting to dance with me but this was an instant NO.

"Sorry Salvador, not even an option baby," I told him.

We exchanged Skype information and moved on our way for the evening. I got to the room and felt like a wet rat. *Gross really, how could he have found me attractive?*

"Salvador was awfully curious about you, Mom," Joseph said.

"Not really, honey. He was just being friendly." I replied and blew off the comment. There were no plans to see Salvador again. I put Joseph to bed and casually sat on the balcony overlooking the ocean. The resort was lit so beautifully. I could hear all the people laughing and talking. I could hear the music in the distance, but over all the noise was the beautiful swishing of the ocean waves.

I wore a tiny tube top dress with flip flops. My body was tan and the tiny white triangles that covered my breasts were contrasted by a beautiful brown glow.

I sipped a glass of wine and enjoyed a little reading when I heard a light knock at the door. In fear of waking my son, I hurried to the door to view out the peephole before opening. I was shocked to see Salvador staring up at me. His eyes were pleading and he was smiling.

I opened the door and immediately put my finger up to my mouth to tell him to be quiet. No words.

He saw me in my little dress and grabbed my waist and pulled me toward him outside the room. He pressed his mouth on mine before I could even say a word. We stood outside my room with the door cracked open by the latch.

The air was hot and tight around us. I tasted cigarettes on his mouth, but his kisses were so intense and hard on my lips that I could hardly think. The light was warm outside my room on the balcony where he pinned me against the wall.

He was whispering to me in Italian, but I couldn't understand a word except for "molto bella."

Everything was going so quickly and we were breathing so heavily. His eyes stared me down as we continued to kiss. Beads of sweat rolled down his face and chest. The light cast a glow on us that made people passing by glance over.

I didn't have a clue what he was saying, but I knew what I was thinking…and it was still a resounding NO.

After moments of wrestling with Salvador, it was time to send the Italian packing. Like I always say, sometimes you just have to leave a good kiss alone.

Cougar? Oh, hell no. This girl don't chase.

Boys & Girls…

You are capable of lying…completely guilt free

You will say anything for sex…anything.

You don't listen, and sometimes we tell you exactly what we want

You don't really tell us how you feel, we can smell your fear.

You are mean to us when you like us

You play games…

You would rather text than pick up the phone;

You love to ask us about the color of our panties.

You don't ask us out, you would rather "meet up" for a drink

You put a good time with your friends before us

You run when things get a little serious.

You avoid serious conversations,

You avoid discussions about the future.

You can't handle the pressure of love

You won't call if we have sex with you on the first date.

You call persistently if you want sex, but haven't gotten it yet;

You get what you want and then you're done.

You are inconsistent;

You send pictures of your man junk 'cause you think it turns us on,

You don't consider kissing cheating

You don't call when you say you will.

You tell us you like us, then treat us badly

You say you miss us but you don't call.

You have so many choices, you can't commit to a date or a time,
You think we will just wait and be available.
We know your phone isn't broken, and you didn't forget to charge it;
We know you are always looking,
We know you don't always use condoms
We know you don't have the mental capacity
to remember important details.
We know you are never really alone;
We know that when you are "single"
it just means you haven't proposed marriage.
You probably have a girlfriend, or two
But it's not all bad.
You are capable of caring,
You are capable of getting swept of your feet.
You can't pretend that having sex with us doesn't matter;
You think about us, more than you will ever admit.
You can't fake a kiss – and it's all in the kiss;
You want someone next to you, but far enough to still be yourself
You just need a little space,
You're a guy and you just need time and space to do your thing.
When you find the ONE, she is the one, there is no mistaking it,
We see how you trip over yourself to be with her.
In that first look you know she is the ONE, and there's not a girl on
this Earth that doesn't dream about that feeling.
And here's the deal about girls…
We are just as full of shit.

Head First

We play games with your head,
We string you along
We expect you to pay…for everything
We think you can read our minds.
We think too much about what your text messages mean,
We wonder why you just don't call when you say you will.
We expect you to open doors,
We judge your gifts and talk to our friends about them.
We don't call you sometimes because we know it scares you,
We overanalyze everything.
We can't really just have sex and walk away;
We talk about your sexual ability, the size of your penis,
And your skill in performing oral sex.
We will claw out our girlfriend's eye to get you, if we want you
We will steal husbands and boyfriends…guilt free.
When we get crazy obsessed with you, we will hack into your email
Looking for something…anything.
We get jealous of your time with your male friends
We can be needy and clingy.
We expect you to know where the clitoris is,
We believe in your lies 'cause they make us feel good.
We want you to tell us we are pretty a million times a day.
We don't really ever want you to acknowledge that we look fat,
We expect you to compliment us without prompting you.
We tell you we don't want flowers, but it's really just a test
To see if you will be gentlemen and buy them anyway.

We will make the mistake of trying
to make you jealous with your friend.
We want you to dress nicely and not embarrass us in public,
But when we love you,
You will never be the same.
The color of your sky will change…forever
And here's what – we both pretty much know
If it's right in the first kiss.
So can we please stop wasting time
with the wrong people and eliminate the bullshit games?

Chapter Thirty-Two

Sexpectations...

Head First

Everybody wants it. It's all about how to get it. What to wear? Where to go? When to do it? How to do it? Who brought the condoms? Who's gonna feel bad tomorrow? Who cares? Who's telling the truth? Who has a girlfriend? Who has a wife? Who has a husband? Who's gonna tell who first?

Men cheat on their girlfriends and their wives. Women cheat on their boyfriends and their husbands. It's all a big mess.

Men tell me they will do "everything but" intercourse because it makes them feel bad. *But hey, a good blowjob is always a nice way to end the work day, right?*

I was surprised at how many men, married or with girlfriends, had absolutely no remorse about asking me out for drinks, texting me, requesting photos, and of course my personal favorite, asking me, "What color are your panties?"

It was exhausting really. But fun as hell at the same time, if you're single anyway. I'm not supporting the marital mess created by infidelity, just so we're clear.

Here is what I've learned about sex: men think about sex a lot…almost all the time. And if they're not getting it in their current relationship, MOST LIKELY, they will get it somewhere else.

Women think about sex too. Although women don't think about it nearly as often as men do, there are some exceptions. Some women, a small fraction, think about sex almost as much as men.

With that being said, here are some other observations. While I can't predict how often some women will be having sex with their boyfriends, man friends or husbands, I can tell that it is in direct proportion to how sexy and attractive she feels.

To get a woman to want sex, you have to be sweet, kind and you have to make her feel sexy. But sometimes the problem is much deeper. Women who have just had babies for example, may feel tired, fat and have saggy, leaky boobs. Guess what? Unless she can somehow turn all of that into a sexy feeling on the inside fellas, you ain't gettin' nothin'.

The woman who continually says, "I feel fat." Guess what? Nothin'. Or if the guy is one of those shit-talking dudes that may have a sexy kitten for a wife, but says stupid things that insult her. Guess what? Nothin'.

Men should really "shut the fuck up" if they can't say something kind to their ladies because, guess what? They aren't getting any. Nothin'.

Even a woman with an inner slut will shut down when she is criticized or belittled.

Some interesting men I've met in the past year have proven my theory. Life, in general, is all about sex. I don't care how old you are, what color your skin is, or how much you weigh, it's the subtext on everyone's mind.

Steven was a handsome man. He was in his late thirties. He was tall, had great, wavy hair and a nice muscular build. He had large strong hands and was overall a very attractive man. We met for coffee after being set up by friends, which I almost always agreed to hesitantly. We met. We liked each other. We decided to have a real date.

The FIRST red flag, (which I never seem to acknowledge), is the point at which I should walk. This is the man who is either too cheap or too horny to take you out on a proper date. *What happened to dinner? What happened to chivalry? Do men really wonder why they are still alone?*

Anyway, Steven talked me into letting him come over to my house where he said we could build a nice fire. He boasted about his fire building capabilities. Then he said we'd order Chinese food and have a nice glass of wine by the fire. *Okay, I'm in.*

It sounded nice, but I'm always hesitant and leery, thinking this is a ploy for sex because it usually is. I had no intention of sleeping with him. But I digress. *So what the hell? I let him come over.*

I wore a white cotton spandex shirt that was a little plunging in the front with long sleeves that clung tight to my arms. It was a pretty hot shirt, the perfect top for a casual date. My jeans were boy cut and my feet were snug in my Uggs. I wore my beloved dog tag and my Coco Mademoiselle.

The SECOND red flag, Steven was almost an hour late. When he finally called to tell me he was running late, he said, "Well, I'm not really that hungry right now, should we wait on the food?" *Are you freaking kidding me? I'm starving!*

"Umm, no, that's not fine." I replied instead. *Stupid, stupid.* "Oh, and I'm bringing some Beer." Steven said. *Gee, thanks, but I don't really drink that much beer and why don't you grab your cowardly balls and ask me what I would like to drink!*

"Well all I have is some frozen vodka and lemons." I told him.

A few moments after we hung up, he arrived. *How could this have happened after a lengthy discussion about the logistics of the evening?*

He piled his beer into the fridge while I sat on my kitchen counter and sipped my vodka. After four sips and no food in my belly, I was already buzzed.

"Do you have any Duraflames logs?" he asked. *No doubt he was getting ready to amass his cave man fire making abilities.*

"Umm…sure I think I have one or two," I plopped off the counter and began my search.

When I came up from the basement with the two logs, Steven was already clearing the mesh cover and getting ready to get the heat going. I sat on the couch and watched closely at his skills. He bent down, put the two Duraflame logs onto the grate, lit them and pulled the mesh cover back over the fire place.

I giggled a little out loud, but roared in my head. *Are you kidding me? THIS was it? A caveman at his finest. Strap a loin cloth on him and I got myself a real alpha male. THIS is the fire? Where's the Chinese food? Where's the wine? He brings over some bullshit beer that I'm certain would never be touched if he left it behind, and that's a really big IF because El Cheapo will sure enough take it back home with him.* Tony Bennett, Norah Jones and John Coltrane played in the background. At least I'd done my part to set the mood.

As Tony Bennett crooned over the nonsense taking place in my home, I realized I didn't care what else happened that night. I was buzzed and warm and all this was pretty damn funny in my head.

The THIRD red flag appeared when he started talking about his ex-wife leaving him because she said she wasn't sexually attracted to him. *What woman divorces a man for that?* If that were really true, this cat had to be terrible in bed.

He didn't appreciate the shocked and smirked look I gave him, but by then the look was plastered on my face like the Joker because of the vodka.

The FOURTH red flag: he hadn't had sex since his divorce because there were "just too many diseases out there." *Shit, I'm out.* I mean, is all this honesty really necessary on a first date? *Jeez pal, slow down on the details, would you?*

He said he wasn't planning on having sex until he was married again. He's like the 40-year-old second time virgin.

This had an exhausting feel to it. Not that I didn't respect his approach to keeping sex special…absofuckinglutely, but really, wouldn't he want to understand compatibility with someone before jumping into marriage? Again? I'm not a shrink, but after the first marriage and all, I don't know, call me crazy.

So as Duraflames burned and the music played softly, I was half crocked and he plowed through beers. He asked me to dance. I was nervous about being on my feet, but what the hell?

The dance started out nicely, very romantic. His strong hands were placed appropriately and we swayed to Norah Jones. Then he came in for a kiss.

With lack of inhibition, I let him kiss me and it was very strong, very aggressive, but also very soft. *I can handle this.*

I also noticed that for a guy abstaining from sex, his hands had begun to move around my hips and waist like he was searching for lost change. His moves sobered me up a little. I grabbed his hands and put them back in place. He looked hurt.

"Sorry dude. I'm just trying to help you keep your promise." He came after me pretty hard there for a minute, but I stumbled my way over to the couch and plopped down like Michael Jordan hitting the bench after playing a rough first half.

Steven walked over and sat next to me. "Will you read your book to me?" I thought that was kind of romantic, so why not?

"Okay," I said. Some of the material was a bit hot and heavy and Steven was really getting into it. It was cute. I felt badly for him because I think his ex did a real number on him. He really seemed like he was timid about getting back on the bike. But I didn't have the energy for this. When Steven left, the Duraflames were but a burnt orange crumble and I stood by the door to bid him adieu. It was about thirty minutes later when the FIFTH and final red flag arose. Tucked into my bed with my LDM by my side and the covers pulled tightly up to my chin, Steven started to text me.

"You are so beautiful and sexy."

"Thank you." I replied back.

"Are you touching yourself? I am." I didn't even respond. I put the phone down, wiped it with antibacterial gel and went to sleep with the vodka induced Joker smirk still plastered to my face.

Chapter Thirty-Three

The Bullshit of all Bullshits…

Love

Head First

It was Friday night. And this weekend I was sans my son. I was invited to a Salsa club But I couldn't find a single person, man, woman or child to go with me. How was that possible? Not one person willing to twirl around for a few hours?

Oh well, that didn't stop me. I fancied up with a beautiful grey dress that hung low in the front and had a slit up the middle by the legs. Just perfect for the sensual Salsa moves. The dress wrapped seductively around my hips and swung when I walked. With my nude stilettos on, I hit the road. I was excited to be going.

When I arrived at the club on Wells, there were very few people there. I almost did the moonwalk outta there before my eyes fell on my friend Mayra. She was my Salsa guru. Mayra planned to put the swing in my hips as long as I was there. After the lessons and the two hours of Salsa dancing, I was laughing, smiling, twirling and really enjoying myself.

The truth about Salsa, in my own, non-trained opinion, is that as long as the man knew what he was doing, then anyone could really do it.

This guy had me spinning and stomping and clapping. I worked up quite a sweat with my newfound friends. After awhile, the music all started to sound the same, but mattered not as I morphed into Gloria Estefan.

The music slowed down and I felt the Latinos' put the sex on me. It was really pretty hot. The Salsa turned into a real book knockin' affair. It felt like they tossed me into an orgy of lovers touching me and pressing their hips on me. It was fun, but the whole affair felt like a workout and made me tired. *Buenos noches.* I was out.

Still early on that Friday night, I meandered to the Red Head Piano Bar, always a good time. Still, sans date, friend or even newfound stranger. But I was not in the bar for three minutes when Jack approached me.

"I'm not sure if you're alone, but if you are, I'd like to talk with you and buy you a drink," he said. *Well, helloooo Jack. Sounded like a good plan to me.*

"I'd like that," I smiled at him. Jack was about six feet tall and in his early forties. His hair was salt and pepper and he was pretty good looking, actually. I gave him TONS of credit for manning up and talking to me as soon as I walked in. *So, what the hell?*

I was up for a yummy dirty martini, so I walked over to the window where he camped out. The Piano Bar was really hopping, tons of people surrounded the pianist and I noticed the piano guy was actually much cuter than my new friend. And he was staring over at me from time to time. *I like this.*

At any rate, Jack and I made small talk over the noise. Then we got out all the usual questions about work. Blah, blah, blah. He wasn't very interesting to be quite honest. He was just a "regular Joe." No molecules rearranged.

Jack did make a few interesting comments that struck me as odd though. Imagine a record playing some miscellaneous nonsense song while I listened to him talk. And then it scratched when Jack started talking crazy. Crazy like how tattoos are for losers. *Ahem, I'm sporting a beauty I designed myself.*

Then he started talking about how he didn't like "Sex and the City" girls. And that it was really a bad idea for people to have dogs. And to top it all off, his Catholic beliefs are paramount in his life. I appreciate and respect people's beliefs. But when they become judgmental it makes me a little queasy.

After an hour or so, Jack decided I was his girlfriend. Apparently somewhere in the last hour, he mustered up the courage and he conjured up the impression that I was his "for the evening" girl, if not for longer. This was unfortunate for me because I was totally digging the piano singer guy, and now I had to get out of this situation. Regardless, Jack reached over to hold my hand during the slow Billy Joel song. *The ever beloved Piano Man…yeesh.* How many times was I going to hear that one during the night?

Jack's hand found mine and without so much as a courtesy squeeze, I sat there on the ledge of the window wondering what the hell Jack was thinking? *How long was I gonna have to keep his hand there? Could I fake a scratch? A nose pick?*

"Excuse me," I pulled my hand out of his and went to the ladies room. But this time I was looking for an out. I didn't want to be roped into talks about the resurrection of Jesus Christ over a dirty martini.

I strolled back to the piano bar and plopped up onto the window ledge and Jack went right on in with the hand-holding thing again. *Ahhh...shit. This ain't gonna be easy.*

As if to avoid this move like I was still in high school, I did a well timed reach for the drink and avoided his grip. The fun fizzled and this guy only wanted to mark his territory, which really annoyed me.

I wrote a little note to the guy singing the tunes. He happened to be friends with Jack, but what the hell? On my note I scribbled: "The girl in the grey dress on the window thinks you're hot." I added my phone number and slid it in between the crowd with their hands swinging to "Hey Jude."

Gag, these oldies were really getting to me. Why in the world did I like this place again? Why did I come here tonight? Note to self: no more Red Head Piano Bar.

"Do you want to go to the back of the bar so we can sit and talk?" Jack asked. *Ughhh…really? Who the hell wants to talk at this time of night?*

"Well, it IS getting late Jack, I should be going." He looked hurt.

"Want to come back to my place and snuggle?" He tried again and came in for a hug and weirdly sniffed my neck. "Mmmm you smell so good it would be so nice to just have you in my arms." Jack closed his eyes and came right over to my face for a kiss. *What? Am I a magnet for douche bags?*

I politely peeled him away, did my famous curtsy and thanked him for a lovely evening. Jack was acting like we were already boyfriend and girlfriend, with his constant need to hold my hand and reaching out with his darting tongue to kiss me. *Bleck!*

"Let me walk you to your car," he persisted.

"Ummm....sure," I said out of a complete knee-jerk reaction. *Shit.*

When I unlocked the car door, Jack put his arms around the top of my shoulders and moved right in for the goodnight kiss. His tongue was darting all over the place like there was peanut butter stuck to the roof of my mouth that he was desperately trying to retrieve. I didn't like it one bit. I rejected the kiss by placing my hand over his mouth.

He looked at me with longing eyes, a big smile and begged to see me again. In fact, he still wanted me to go home and snuggle with him.

Why I gave him my number earlier that evening was perplexing to me. I really needed to think more seriously about that...bad idea.

Jack texted me before I got home. He told me how pretty I looked and how much he missed me already. *Ugh, a "stage 5 clinger" for sure.*

Out of curiosity, I had to understand how this guy was wired. So I talked to him a few times. He seemed to have women stereotyped. He was alone in his forties and I never questioned why.

"Can I please see you again?" He begged.

"Well, I'm going to this new Asian restaurant called Sunda that I'm blogging about so if you want, you can meet me and my friends there." At this point, it was all about research. I was curious about him, curious how a man could be so damn needy, so clingy. Had he been that badly burned by another woman, or was he just weird?

Jack groaned. "Oh…ummm…sometimes my stomach gets kind of nervous on first dates so maybe I should just meet you after dinner." He replied to my suggestion. *Whaaaaat????? Are you freaking kidding me? Dare I say, another El Cheapo?*

"Really? I mean really, Jack? You seemed very comfortable putting your tongue in my mouth the other night, so didn't we pass the first date thing already?" I was aggravated. "So how exactly does that work, Jack?" I raised my voice.

"Can I be honest?" He asked.

"No, please lie to me, that feels so much better, DUH."

"See, I get real tired of spending money on dinners and drinks when women never offer to pay, and don't so much as say 'thank you' afterwards, let alone give you a good night kiss." Jack tried to explain.

"Hmmm, so you don't want to make the investment without a guaranteed return?" was all I could ask.

"Well, yes," he said. "These women today are all so 'Sex and the City' with their little dogs and their high expectations."

But the truth of the matter is, he was entirely wrong with his ideas about SOME women today, but to throw out a lie like his stomach gets nervous? Bullshit – that is the bullshit of ALL bullshits. *I'm out. Cheap, crazy, broke and opinionated…this guy was the Mayor of Desperate Town, population ONE.*

After that, I briefly dated an artist. He was cool. I loved his intrinsic creativity. He was pensive and methodic. His work was beautiful.

We were just getting to know each other. We'd been on a couple of dates. But deep down, I knew he was not right for me. I wanted him to be right. I liked the idea of him. Yet, I thought I should give it more time to let some things unfold and see where it took us.

So after two weeks, he told me he loved me. *How in the hell was that possible?*

He wanted to call me his girlfriend after one date. He wanted to do sleep-overs the first week. He wanted to be my son's friend. *Oh hell no. Pump the brakes man.*

He was needy. He was clingy. He wanted to skip right over the "get to know you phase" and have a key to my home. *Ugh…this is the bullshit of all bullshits!*

Chapter Thirty-Four

Sweet, Sweet Michael...

Love

I attempted to end things with Michael as part of my New Year's resolution. That last about a week.

I attempted to let him go again in the spring, which lasted about three weeks. When summer came and he began to wrap up his MBA, I thought for sure it was time to go our separate ways.

This time it lasted six weeks, mostly because he had exams and I was going through some shit at work that kept me sufficiently distracted.

I was happy with Michael. I really didn't want to end things with him so I stopped threatening to break up with him every other day.

We were together often and it was perfect. As we rounded a year and a half of being together, it was apparent just how difficult it was going to be to let go.

For my birthday, Michael came over late one night without calling first. He had a huge bouquet of flowers, Gerber Daisies, my favorite. He walked into my home as he had so many times before. His smile lit up his face and mine too.

I missed him. It had only been a few days since I last saw him, but I missed him.

I never wanted Michael to be something he wasn't. I always knew our relationship was temporary and nothing more than the physical intimacy we shared. There was a deep appreciation and love growing that was a gift, but I realized it would soon be time to give him up. For real. For sure. Forever.

"Happy birthday sweetheart," he whispered onto my neck and into my ear.

We stood in my bedroom like so many times before. The song "Mad" by Ne-Yo played in the background and he spun me around to look at me in the mirror. "You are so beautiful," he said. We looked at each other.

He smiled at me. I turned to him, unable to resist his lips. Our eyes met and our lips touched lightly. We kissed each other softly on the neck.

There were plenty of times we were together where it was all about playing, it was fun and it was crazy hot. This time was different.

This time reminded me I needed to let him go. We both deserved more, but those moments we fit together perfectly and neither one of us wanted it to end.

We were getting closer to our ending.

I suspected that once he became engrossed in his business career, which always lent itself to the possibility of moving, it would just dissolve on its own. My friends were envious of my relationship with Michael. They all thought it was so hot that he was so young. To me though, it was just something that happened. We didn't seek each other out because of our ages, it was just that damn chemistry. And over a year later, it was still going strong.

As Maya Angelou once wrote, "A woman should have a past juicy enough that she's looking forward to retelling it in her old age." I got your back Maya.

Chapter Thirty-Five

You Can't Fake It... Love

Head First

I walked out on a guy because I didn't like his feet. Everything was going great. He was funny, nice-looking, responsible, and smart. We had a good time.

We were at his house and he fired up the hot tub to take a little dip. I could tell he had orchestrated the entire evening to perfection. My favorite cabernet, the hot tub, and The Phantom of the Opera music (I'm still not sure about that one though).

Regardless, I was in the bathroom changing into a bikini. But when I stepped out in his robe, he was all ready to go…and I do mean ready to go. I glanced down at his feet and noticed quite possibly the most unkempt feet I had ever seen. The nails were long, with some discoloration, and the bottoms looked like scratchy skateboards. There was a yellowish color and, dare I say, dirt under the nails which grossly extended past his finger-like digits.

A well timed record scratch interrupted the music and I looked down almost in horror.

"Gia, what's wrong?" he asked quickly with concern.

"Ummm, I, uhhh, nothing,…" I responded as I looked down at the second toe and noticed it was all banged up and overlapping it's neighborly, innocent bystander next to it. I was actually grimacing.

"Hey, umm, just give me a second, OK?" I said as I ran back into the bathroom. I sat on the ledge of the tub to process this new information. OK, nice guy, responsible, good looking – PRO. But disgusting feet – CON.

Enough contemplation. "I'm out," I said to myself. I didn't like his feet. I could picture them rubbing up against my well pedicured tootsies and I almost gagged. I could almost feel them skimming and scratching my leg. *This date was over.*

I stepped out of the bathroom fully dressed. Now he was the one who looked shocked. "I'm having stomach problems and I need to leave." I just wasn't feeling well – and in fact, that was no lie.

I let another one go because the hair on his arms was too puffy. He was older and classy, had a good job, blah, blah, blah. But all I could think about was petting his arms. While his lips moved and he jabbered on and on, I couldn't help but wonder if that hair spread rampantly across his chest and, dare I say, his back? *Yeesh.* The thought of it made me cringe. I couldn't take any chances here either. I was out. Not for me.

And then there was the "funny walking man." We were on a date Downtown with my four-inch heels, and they were killing my feet. They were shoe booties entering the scene for the first time. My date insisted on walking from Rush and Oak Street to Hubbard Street. *Holy Shit.* My dogs were barking, but I manned up, bit the bullet, and strutted my strutter.

What I found weird and most annoying was that he chose to walk behind me and put his arms around me so we were walking in lock step with each other. *What the hellllll?* I felt like we were doing that old walk from the Monkeys… *"Here we come…walking down the street…hey, hey, we're the Monkeys…"* How was it possible that he thought this was comfortable, or even remotely pleasant for me? AS IF I wanted a 240 pound man adding weight to my already bubbled up blisters and raw heels.

Gently, with my pinky up, I released the weight of his arms from my shoulders. "Can you walk beside me?" I asked him.

"Sure," he said. The swing in his walk was a bit like Quasimodo dragging a bag of laundry. THIS was worse and attracted more attention than was necessary on a Saturday at midnight on Rush Street. *Oh, Christ…I was out.* "TAXI!"

As if I'd been out on dates with the entire city of Chicago, or so it felt, not in the slutty kind of way, just the first date kind of way. But I firmly believed Mr. Right would not find me while sitting on the couch shoveling popcorn into my mouth and watching reruns of Forgetting Sarah Marshall or Superbad – two movies my girlfriends swore they would confiscate if I watched them even one more time.

But I couldn't resist James. He was tall, handsome and talented. He didn't make me laugh. And I'm pretty sure we weren't exactly compatible, but he was sexy as hell. *I'm only human, right?* Indeed he was sexy. Yada, yada, yada. But that's all I got.

Or how about any of these: Guy who constantly talked about his parents? Guy who talked about his ex-girlfriends and how HOT they were? Or how about the guy who dressed nicely over-all, but when I looked down at his feet, he was wearing deck shoes (like deck shoes from the early nineties when men actually wore deck shoes)? I mean, was he cheap? Did he believe they still looked new? Had he not picked up a GQ magazine? EVER?

And let's talk about "manscaping." This topic had men whipping out razors, using creams, waxing, and God knows what else. We love it. We really do appreciate the attention to detail. We love escaping the embarrassment of stray hairs, you know that one hair that suddenly appears. This is NOT sexy. We all know the hair is there. We know that if we kiss we may just pass it back and forth so we do the old finger sweep to get rid of the little bastard and then we're back to business.

So the general thesis of the topic is that WE LOVE IT and we appreciate the uncomfortable risks you must take with that razor. HOWEVER, could you please tell ALL your friends that manscaping is no longer optional, it is required.

Additionally, when something from the 1980s appears on any part of a man, ladies are OUT. Step into the 21st Century.

So what am I saying? It's simple. NONE OF THOSE GUYS WERE RIGHT FOR ME. In a hundred percent of the cases, I knew it in the first ten minutes. There was something in my gut screaming at me, but I refused to listen.

I was a hopeless romantic. I wanted to give all these lovelies a try in case I overlooked something amazing. But you can't fake chemistry. You can't fake love. When it's right, all the bullshit falls away. I would give him a pedicure or a back waxing, I could do the manscaping myself or I could beg him to brush his teeth. But love? Well…you can't get that in a tube of toothpaste.

The feet, the hair, the breath, or anything else is just the final reason we find to leave a relationship. Subconsciously, we need an escape route. With the right man, none of that matters.

Chapter Thirty-Six

On that Note... The Wrap Dress...

I've seen friends end up in this place. I've not actually experienced it myself in the past two years since my divorce, but I was staring right down the fork in the road.

I met him during one of my food blogging experiences. On paper, he was perfect. If dating were like hiring, he would probably already have the job, but it's really quite different.

Certain qualifications are important, so we don't make the same mistakes over and over again. They are only one part though, one clue to the mystery and one piece of the puzzle.

Josh was tall, good-looking, had a great job, nice dresser and was a smart guy. I went on one date, two dates, three dates, had lots of kisses and found myself running for the door one month in, when he told me he loved me.

AS IF I hadn't learned ANYTHING. So what happened? Well, it was simple. He was just not right for me. He wanted a girlfriend. I thought I wanted a boyfriend. He did all the things the other guys failed to do. He sent the perfect text. He was honest with his feelings. He was available. He loved to talk on the phone and have long, intense conversations. He liked to walk in the park, hand in hand. He was affectionate. He was loving. He was really into me. He wanted to meet my friends. He wanted to meet my family and he wanted to meet my son Joseph. And yes, while it was all so damn fast he was, as I say, perfect on paper.

When I told my friends about him they were so happy for me. I wanted him to be right. I was in love with the idea of him, but I was not in love with him, not even close. So there was the fork. I could, like some women I know, keep him as my boyfriend. I could allow him to believe we had a future, leading him to believe that I really loved him. And I could try to convince myself that I loved him.

But what I wanted more was the Va-va-voom. I wanted the feeling of standing next to someone who just made my molecules rearrange. I wanted to feel his energy from across the room. I wanted to feel uncomfortably, unthinkably, distracted by his smile, his smell and his touch. And I wasn't.

In fact, the longer I tried, the more dates I went on, the more I realized that. He just wasn't the right guy for me. He wasn't the "one." The best thing I could do was to be honest and move on. I did. I told him the truth. I couldn't make the same mistake twice, not a chance. He deserved more and so did I.

I chose the path less traveled. Many women I know would rather have this fine looking man on their arm than no man at all. But I was okay with it though. I knew exactly what I wanted. I knew what my heart was willing to wait for. What I deserved.

Josh was like a wrap dress. I admire wrap dresses. They looked lovely on the hanger and I tried them on almost every time I went shopping. Every single time, 100% of the time, I found myself looking in the mirror with the exact same expression, "It's beautiful, but it's not me."

Chapter Thirty-Seven

Never Enough of New York...

Head First

For years, I had a great friend in New York, whom I loved dearly. He was a very important vascular surgeon, but to me he was just Jean (Jean, pronounced like Jean-Claude Van Damme). I met him years earlier.

We developed a friendship immediately. He was French and he spoke four different languages. He was six foot four with jet black hair and a thin frame. He had the most perfect nose and large brown eyes. He was handsome and his accent was unmistakably sexy. He was ten years older than me. He had VIP patients all over the world and his work kept him traveling constantly.

He was separated from his wife and had a very respectable relationship with his family. He was a dedicated father and always gave his free time to his children.

We had known each other for years. There was always the question of more than friendship; but of course during my marriage, that was not a possibility, failing as it was.

However, we bonded immediately and we became good friends. He saw something in me that most people didn't bother to see. He saw that I was strong, independent, sensual; but he also saw that I could be fragile and vulnerable, like a little girl. He was drawn to me and I loved that he saw those sides in me. Most men didn't get past the strong part.

I only saw Jean a few times a year, because he lived in New York. He was an amazing person. He was brilliant, snobby, picky and arrogant at times, but I saw through all of that. I loved him for who he was. He was nurturing and generous and had a big heart. Jean flew Joseph and I to New York City over the Summer of 2009 and we had the most amazing weekend at the Marriott Marquis in Times Square. Joseph will never forget that trip.

Jean took care of all the expenses. That's just the way he was. He actually had to fly out and see a patient in France that weekend so he couldn't spend any time with us.

Joseph and I spent hours at Central Park, FAO Schwartz, took a rickshaw to St. Patrick's Cathedral; and of course we took the ferry to Ellis Island and the Statue of Liberty. We stayed up watching On Demand movies until two in the morning. It turned out to be a priceless weekend.

So many times I traveled to New York to see Jean. He was always there whisking around, seeing patients and having sushi with me.

For my birthday, he surprised me with a trip to New York City for the weekend. Joseph was with his dad, so it was just me flying in. When my plane landed at LaGuardia, everything I loved about New York flooded through.

I hadn't seen him since earlier that year in Chicago. It seemed all the previous times he visited, I was melancholy; I was always in flux with my emotions, but this time was different. I was on top of the world – this was my time.

The first call I got from him was, "Honey I have bad news." *Hmmm…that had become so predictable over the past few years.* I respected his work and what he had to do. He was not able to spend as much time with me as he originally thought.

We met for lunch and Nobu. His big brown eyes stared at me the whole time.

"So tell me honey, how are you?" He asked with a big smile as his eyes clung to my lips.

"I'm great, and it's so wonderful to see you." It was the truth. I loved being with him.

"Tell me, how is Joseph?" Again he was, enraptured by my every word.

"You look so beautiful, love, just gorgeous." He said with admiration.

All I could do was stare back with a smile that told him everything. He had a little time before going to the hospital, so we walked down Fifth Avenue and did some shopping.

It was delightful. I enjoyed being with him. I was the only person he could just let it down with; he didn't have to impress me. I listened to his conversations where he would switch between three different languages: English, French and Arabic, all in one conversation. It just made me smile.

He admired my talent, my strength and my beauty. He always told me so. I shopped on Fifth Avenue, stopped into St. Patrick's Church to light a candle, and plowed my way through Times Square. It was a delicious day.

We planned to meet up for a late dinner, so I had a few hours to kill. I attended the Bikram Studio class on Eighth Avenue. Dedicated to my ever ass-kicking Bikram Yoga, I spent the next 90 minutes in hell. When it was over, I walked back to The Alex Hotel the long way. I passed Times Square.

It all felt different now, or maybe it was just me that was different. I was happier. I could see things more clearly. I didn't carry all the stress I had in previous visits to this city.

Jean saw it in me as well. I celebrated it. I deserved it. I was all dolled up in my little black dress that night when I got the call he had to run to the hospital for surgery. I sat in my dress and breathed a sigh of disappointment.

I scooped myself up and headed out to dinner on my own. There wasn't a chance I was going to sit in my hotel room. The LBD (little black dress) needed to take a test drive.

I headed to my favorite restaurant, Chin Chin, where I knew the owner and I always got rock star service. Jimmy greeted me with open arms. This place was home to professional athletes and celebrities. But tonight, Jimmy made me feel like I was the only celebrity around. He cleared out a special table just for me and the wine began flowing. It was an incredible night. The other patrons kept looking over to see who I was and what all the fuss was about.

Halfway through my meal, a beautiful woman who was with her boyfriend approached me. He looked like A-Rod and she looked something like Mariah Carey actually.

When her boyfriend went to the restroom she waved me over to her table as if there was something wrong and she needed to tell me.

"Hi, are you OK?" I asked with care and curiosity.

"Yes, I'm fine, but could you please give me your phone number?" She asked quickly.

"Umm…sure. Are you OK?" Once again I asked just in case there might be something wrong.

"No baby, I'm fine. I will text you in a minute, OK?" was all she said.

"Oh, OK, sure," and I gave her my number and returned to my seat in confused curiosity.

As soon as they left, I got a text message from her immediately that said I was "hot and beautiful" and that she wanted to "pleasure me" with her boyfriend watching.

I've seen this text before. *Holy shit…this night's getting interesting.*

I politely declined. She kept texting me the entire night. It was flattering, but nothing more.

I told Kim, my waiter, about it and I could hear him repeating my story in Chinese to the other staff. He was a much older, smaller, wonderful Asian man. "You like me walk you to corner?" Kim asked with a strong accent.

"Yes Kim. That would be nice," I said. It was getting late and the extra added security was comforting.

"OK, you meet me on corner in ten minutes," he waved and pointed to the street.

"You got it Kim, thank you." I said good-bye to Jimmy and thanked him for the great service.

We met on the corner and walked a few blocks and then he decided to walk me all the way to the hotel, which got me wondering if Kim was going to be expecting something else. After all, this night had an unpredictable spin to it.

"OK Gia, you take care now," he said and reached over to give me a hug, which was fine. However, the hug turned into an eager attempt for a kiss on the mouth, which was just NOT going to happen. *What the hell was going on here?* I politely turned away and smiled.

I ran into the Ringo Bar in the hotel. The bartender was cleaning up.

"Hey man, how are you? Can I please get a glass of Chardonnay?" I said almost short of breath. "On second thought, I'll take the whole bottle!"

He agreed but looked at me with curiosity.

"It's been an eventful night." Feeling like I needed an alibi or something, I told him about what happened. The bartender laughed his ass off, "Well, you are looking pretty fine in that dress. What are you doing later?" *Really? Seriously? Grrrrrr, I'm out!* OK, the LBD was hot, I can't deny, or maybe it was my new $40 vanilla lotion from Henri Bendel? Either way, there was something in the air that night.

I waited an hour for Jean. With all the wine, I was getting sleepy. It was sad to think the whole city had seen me in my pretty dress, but not the man I wore it for.

I went back to the hotel room. I set my glass down at the bedside. There were candles burning and Diana Krall played softly in the background.

I woke to Jean's kiss on my forehead. I opened my eyes and he was in his scrubs, but looking as handsome as ever. He kissed me gently and raised me up to twirl me around in my pretty little black dress. I felt like the tiny dancer in the jewelry box. He brought a dozen red roses with him and had taken off some of the petals and scattered them all over the bed, and on me. "You are a rose, darling." He said.

We swayed softly to the music. I put my sleepy head on his shoulder. I didn't have to pretend with him. I didn't have to be anything but me. It was always good enough for him.

He kissed me softly on the lips, but nothing more. It just wasn't who we were.

We lay together with the rose petals around us and the sounds of New York were muted for just a few moments.

When I woke in the morning, still in my LBD, there was a note on the pillow next to me which read, "Always loving you." Jean was my almost lover.

Chapter Thirty-Eight

Enough...

Head First

I have never felt stronger, healthier and more at peace with myself. They said this would happen. I believed it because I was there, at the age of knowing who I am.

I took time to reflect on the past couple of years and all the things that had occurred over the past decade.

I was happier now, but there were still times of sadness. And there were also times when laughter was so hard it actually hurt, but in between there was just peace.

I had come to believe peace could only come when the voice inside me was stronger than the voices around me. Judgment and fear were like monsters and once they were no longer invited or welcomed, I could live my life the way I wanted to.

As my own Declaration of Independence, I declared my life would be intentional and have direction, provided by my own instincts. I would be lead by what was in my heart.

NO ONE could know what is there. No one could predict my journey or even pretend to understand it. I found it was even important for me to stop judging others as well.

How many times had I pretended to know how to give advice to someone when I had no real clue what their lives were about? Who was I to be doing this? ENOUGH. Enough. That was all that resonated in my head. How many times had I heard my son would be "fine" after the divorce? Or heard, "you need to stop doing this, or that" or "you need to do this with your money" or "you need to go here, or there." MY NAME IS NOT UNITA (as in YouNeedTa).

How many people had walked in my shoes? How many people had gone through my childhood? How many people buried their fathers at the age of 26? How many people moved ten times in twelve years? How many people had miscarriages? How many people went through in vitro fertilization three times in a row only to be disappointed and heartbroken?

How many people sat their children down to tell them their family was splitting up? How many people sat without their children on Christmas Day because it was the other parent's day? How many people carried my burdens? How many people dealt with the ever burdening sadness of divorce on a child?

How many people went to work with tears behind their eyes because their child was not doing well? How many people could feel my loneliness when they were out with their husbands on "date night?"

Likewise, how many people had the skills and talents that were within me? How many people had the perseverance to get up, over and over, when life had me down? How many people had friends so dear and so near that they would drop everything to be at each other's sides in times of need?

How many people dream big enough dreams that people actually laugh at them?

No one else had this story. No one else had my power or energy. No one else had anything like me, so how could they possibly judge me? How could I even begin to think they would understand? And, in truth, how could I judge them?

I have had ENOUGH of this bullshit. I've had enough of people judging my hair, make-up, clothes, shoes, tattoos, piercings, language…how many men I date, or how I parent my child, where I go, how long I stay, with whom I go, or whatever else I choose to do in this world. ENOUGH.

I mean really, didn't people have anything better to talk about and do? Why was my world so important that they couldn't focus on their own?

If you can love me and accept me, well…that's just good enough for me. And in return, I will do the same. Plain and simple.

So, as part of this Declaration, I say to you, who are so beautiful inside and out, declare it now. No more bullshit. Haven't we all had ENOUGH?

Chapter Thirty-Nine

My sweet little boy: Words could never describe how my heart broke the day I told you that your dad and I were getting a divorce. If I could have spared you that pain, I would have. If I could have left your life untouched by fear or stress, or sadness from this, baby I would have. If I could have gone on believing that my happiness in this world was not important, I would have.

If I could have dried every tear you shed with my own kisses and hugs and covered your ears to every argument, I would have. If I could have taken away your pain, your sadness, your disappointment in me, I would have. If I could have gone through this world thinking you were the only one I needed, I would have. But I couldn't. And I can't.

I carried you inside me and brought you into this world, but I can't pretend my own existence disappeared the day you were born. I love you with every inch of my body and soul. We are one heart.

And now, as I've listened to your anger at me, your disappointment with my choices, and your hatred for the changes in your life, I have heard your words and watched you slam your fists around. I am broken-hearted. And baby boy, I get it. I do. This sucks for you. This sucks for all of us.

And there are times, like right now, that I am without you, missing the sweet sound of your voice. I'm missing your breath on my neck when we snuggle at night. I'm missing your sweet embrace telling me you love me. I'm missing our arguments about drinking milk and eating vegetables. Yes, I miss you more than you will ever know. My heart is with you always and time will never make this feel better. Time will never fill the void that exists in my heart when you're not with me. Missing a single "good night" breaks my heart.

I sometimes sit in your room and just smell your pillow because I miss you so much. I miss my sweet little boy.

I find myself driving and listening to our favorite songs, thinking you are in the back seat smiling at me with those delicious cheeks and happy eyes.

Sometimes when it's quiet, I forget you are gone and find myself whispering on the phone because I think you're here sleeping. Crazy, huh? Love will do that to you.

Baby boy you may never know in this life how deep my love goes for you. You may never know the things I went through to make your life a happy one. You may never know how many times I cried for you, just wanting your happiness. You may never know how many times I begged God to take away your tears and pain and burden me with all your worries.

You may never know to what lengths I hurried, scurried and hustled just to be at your side, or how I tried to protect you from pain of any kind.

You may never know how hard I tried to make you smile when you were sad, and how much I wanted your life to be perfect.

You may never know how many times I stayed awake at night just to make sure the tooth fairy would come or how many times I lay awake and watched you sleep, and shed tears of joy, just looking at the rise and fall of your chest.

You may never know how many prayers I said out loud to God while you slept at my side. But God knows…He was watching. He was listening. And He was protecting you.

I hate these times without you. They are the worst. So I must wait. You will return home and life will feel normal again. My arms will be waiting and we will be together.

So young man, let me tell you something about life: Stuff happens to you. It does. And believe it or not, this will not be the worst thing that happens in your life. Your heart will be broken again, perhaps many times. Your dreams will seem shattered. Your life will seem confusing and unthinkably difficult.

But here's what, here's what I am going to tell you: It's not what happens to you in life. It's what YOU do when it happens. I can tell you that we prayed together every night with complete faith that God had given us each enough strength to get through the difficult times.

Each night, I used to whisper in your ear, "What is impossible with God?"

You whispered back to me, "Nothing Mama…nothing." Never forget that sweetheart. Nothing is impossible with God. He is always there. He can change your life in the blink of an eye. He is as close as your next breath, your next heart beat. Don't ever forget the power of your faith. Remember that God has you right where He wants you and will never leave you alone in times of sorrow or stress. Give Him praise in the good times and the bad and you will always feel Him in your heart.

You got through this. You most certainly did. We prayed together. We cried together. We lived life together and we got through it all.

And truly, if I could have found another way to show you just how brave, courageous and strong you are, I would have. If I could have taught you life lessons without breaking your heart, I would have. If I could have chosen any other path to lead you to the wonderful person you are today, I would have. Your life has made you wonderful. Your life has taught you lessons. Your life is grand.

Remember that. ALWAYS remember that.

And know this: I ALWAYS loved you…ALWAYS believed in you…and I ALWAYS will.

All My Love, Mom

Chapter Forty

Head First

I am responsible for my own life, my own happiness.

I intend to make mistakes. I intend to get messy. I intend to learn and grow. My plan is to find new ways to use what God has given me.

I am beautiful, I am amazing, and so are you. Everyone has something to offer. Everyone has a gift to share that has been given only to them.

I intend to use every last drop of talent, every last drop of grace, every last drop of love, every last drop of courage. There will be nothing left.

I refuse to die with the music still in me. I will have wrinkles to show all the suns I have seen rise so high in the sky across city streets, the blue oceans, my little boy's eyes, and over my father's grave.

My body may be tired one day but my spirit will always fly, always be soaring, always reaching for new heights.

My heart may be heavy for all the things I've pretended not to worry about or be afraid of. It may have been broken a million times, but you know what they say about a muscle: it can only grow once stretched beyond its normal capacity.

My heart carries love and compassion, and yet there is always room for more. There are always more ways to love, to be a blessing to others.

I may not have all the answers, but I have learned how to ask. Most importantly, I've learned how to listen to the voice that guides me…directs me…protects me.

I have laughed a million laughs, so hard I've cried. I have

endured tickle fights that are more meaningful than job promotions.

I have stopped in my tracks to stare at the moon. I have watched it follow me and felt its glowing wonder; thinking, feeling, believing that it's brightness would illuminate my path.

I wouldn't trade a single step of this adventure…it's all mine. Once you realize that life is an adventure, not a journey, you can lighten the burden of worry, fear and judgment. You can be liberated knowing that all things have a purpose, and are part of the magnificent plan of your life.

It was and forever will be…my life…my choice.

Laugh with me. Cry with me. Make mistakes with me. It's okay…there is a plan for it all. Believe. Have faith. Never stop thinking that you are divine. Most importantly, please make a promise to yourself that you will ALWAYS believe in your greatness; that you will NEVER give up on your dreams; that you will always believe that anything is possible…anything.

"When I go to meet the Lord, I want to be able to say to Him, Lord, I used everything you gave me." Erma Bombeck.

Head First

Paper Hearts

I have been up forever watching the moon,
Listening for the stars to sing or dance,
Searching the night sky for answers to my questions,
I don't mind the darkness.
Darkness means there is one more chance...
Before tomorrow,
I can still love,
I can still cry,
I can still hurt,
I can still ask why.

I will take my chances and pass for tonight;
I draw it big and cast my heart onto the starry sky.
Like a child's artwork on the wall
I scribble it red for love, blue for pain,
But no one really knows at all.
I am the artist of my life
I dream it big and throw my world into chance;
Like a blank canvas in the sky,
I swirl a rainbow for luck and a heart for love,
But there is no luck only reasons why.

Reasons why we do the things
That makes us laugh or cry.
Never wanting to change a thing
The memory is what we hold tight.

And it's all about the memory
Color it. Dream it. Make it. Love it.
Make only the ones you will love,
Lose the ones that cause you pain.
Draw them black and throw them into the night sky.
Turn your back and see the twinkle of the stars,
Just for you, before tomorrow.
Darkness gives you one more chance.
You can choose your color,
Choose your dream,
Choose your memory.
Make it so big it will make you dance for hours and sing for years.
Live it full and smile for a lifetime.
Choose to let the darkness change your heart.
Draw it big and cast it onto the night.
Before tomorrow.

Chapter Forty-One

How Do You Do It?

Love

How do you start your life over? How do you go from one set of habits and routines to another? Do you need to change everything or just some things? Do you keep the same friends? Do you find new ones? Do you go back to school? The possibilities are endless, but the answer is simple.

The first thing you have to do is get rid of all the bullshit that you've been telling yourself. All the lies that make you feel insignificant, that you're not enough, or that you don't deserve better. Then decide what kind of life you really want to have, decide what you REALLY want. Then get off your ass and stop talking about it. Don't think, just do it. You follow your gut. All the answers are there, without fail.

It had been almost two years since my divorce. Older and wiser, I wanted more for my life. When I first came back to Chicago, I had one friend, my beloved AJ, no social life, no direction, and I knew it was time to turn it all around.

I got after it. I decided to cultivate my passion for writing and attempted to write anything for anybody that would read it. Before long, I found people begging me to send them something to read. They wanted to hear more of the story. It made them feel close to their own truth.

I also decided it was time to find some friends. Friends that I could really think of as friends, not just those people you call when you're bored.

But I also took the time to really think and evaluate what makes ME happy and what brings me joy. I wanted more of it. But it wasn't selfish. It was the right thing to do. I could only be a good mother when I myself was in a good place. In order for all my relationships to succeed, I had to have a good one with myself. *Cliché?* Maybe, but when you follow your heart, it's like you're not working another day in your life.

Despite my past experience with Match.com, I got involved with Facebook, Twitter, and any other form of social media that I could use to find an audience. I sought people on Facebook that looked interesting and asked them out for coffee. I wanted to surround myself with people who were amazing, who had dreams, ambitions, great energy, and were fun to be with.

I found a connection with a food website(www.eFete.net) and negotiated my way into writing a weekly food blog about dating and dining in Chicago, appropriately titled "About Last Night." I met so many interesting people through this writing. DC Crenshaw, who ran the website, was a tall, talented, ex-football player, and we mutually supported each other. I wrote for him religiously, and we supported each other's work. Everywhere I went, I talked about the writing, sending chapters, and meeting interesting people who wanted to help with my writing endeavors.

I was continually amazed at how the right people just kept moving into my life, but they were not accidents. They were all part of the plan. I knew that plan was to write. It was time to follow my heart. My life coach, sweet Alberto, would tell me that every day I needed to wake up and yell three times, "Fuck fear, fuck fear, FUCK FEAR," with each time being louder than the next, followed by "I am following my heart." You'd be surprised how liberating that was. I'm sure my neighbors thought I was a little crazy, but you know… well, I am. Fear does not live in my home. I will not allow it.

I met a new friend at Caribou Coffee one morning because he was an event planner and I wanted to discuss some things with him post book launch. I was running late.

After greeting him, I went to grab my Espresso. While waiting in line, I almost literally bumped into this woman who was in a slight panic and appeared stressed.

I politely introduced myself as she looked interesting. She said she was a clothing designer and she was having a premier event to launch her new line that night so she was freaking out. Her eyes were racing but she looked beautiful. She looked me up and down in a casual, interesting way and said, "Who are you? You look like somebody!"

Well indeed she was right, damn it…I AM SOMEBODY! I assured her that I would be at her party to support her that night.

Not a single friend in tow, as they were all locked into other plans, I dressed myself up on a Friday night and headed to Lumen for her fashion launch. I worked my way right into the VIP section and sat with her staff, modeling agents, photographers and other interesting people. It was a very cool experience. I managed to find myself a photographer and a date all in a few hours. Not to mention, the very next day I sailed into her store to secure some key pieces for my wardrobe. I prefer to call shopping "character development." It was wonderful. This lady was amazing and I was now a part of her world, and she was now a part of mine. How cool was that?

I met new people all the time. I forced myself into uncomfortable situations because I knew it would be good for me. I met people at yoga. I met people on the street, restaurants, bars, grocery stores. I introduced myself to the world because it was full of amazing people.

Sure I had fear. Sure there were times that my forty dollars worth of Chinese food and On-Demand TV was a good night. Everybody needs that once in awhile. But I've said this before: everything you want is right outside your comfort zone.

I pushed and stretched, and I shared my passions with the world. I got back into making jewelry and sold pieces right off my neck.

I would Fed Ex chapters of my book to news anchors just to see if they would read them. I shared my gifts and found that people really did want to be a part of me…my writing…my jewelry…my life.

It was almost completely different now. This was the life I had created. It was healthy, it was fun, it was crazy, and it was a little racy. It was certainly not predictable.

People teased me because, as a mother first, I can be June Cleaver baking cookies one minute and Rhianna the next, with my short, crazy hair and smoked out eye makeup.

So what? Our ability to shift our lives and be flexible with the Universe is critical to our success in life.

There are no shortcuts. All of this takes time, but you have to dream big and you have to be listening for the direction. It's all there. That's how you do it.

Chapter Forty-Two

It Took a Little Time...

Head First

It took a little time. Sometimes it takes a gallon of sorrow and a bucket of tears but one day, one sunny day, you look up and realize that you're not crying anymore. You realize you've laughed more in one day that you had in an entire year.

You no longer spend your days looking through the rear view mirror, but the view directly in front of you takes you exactly where you need to go.

Sure, you find yourself wondering, "How did I get here?" and "How the hell did I make it through all that shit?" And the answer is…it doesn't even matter. You just did it.

You look at your child whom you would have thought would never smile again, and he's laughing and loving life. In fact, you see a look of love and happiness on his face. Once again, you are reassured that you do know just what you're doing. Not only are these beautiful souls resilient, they are full of love and know how to love under all circumstances and through all conditions.

This is what I know about me: I am amazing. I've come to learn we're all amazing. I am only just beginning to understand all the talents and possibilities in my life. I am just now understanding what it means to really love myself, and my life.

I am forever touched by the pain. Thank God. I am forever loved by the countless people who walk this journey with me. I am full of possibilities and have a lifetime to see them through.

I am beautiful, inside and out. I am done being judged. I am deliberate and intentional. I am free of all that binds me to pain and worry, AND SO ARE YOU.

I choose laughter. I choose love and it chooses me. My life has eternal significance, AND SO DOES YOURS.

You are amazing and your light burns so brightly. If I met you and looked you in the eye, I would tell you that you are beautiful.

I would tell you that your spirit is so big, it fills a room. I would tell you to never give up on yourself. I would tell you that anything is possible.

I would want you to know that your life is significant. You would feel my love.

I would tell you to never be out of the fight. I would tell you to jump HEAD FIRST into your life. No fear. There is no other way.

From My Sweet Baby Boy…

My Mom was going through tough times with me. And she got through it, so this book is kinda hopeful. It's an adventure of things we went through together. So if I helped her and she helped me…well she wrote this book to be inspirational. The things I like about my Mom are that she is very nice and sweet, and she is always there for me. So if you have trouble with your children, this is a good book for you to read.

Acknowledgments

Alberto, you helped me find Gia. You are a blessed soul and you called my bullshit. Thank you for coaching me back into life – a life I love.

Angel sister Jill, you showed me love; you gave me the gift of great friendship and you were a source of strength when I needed it most. I love you dearly.

Annaliese, you showed me how to give it all up, how to create my own future and find my Dad. You were there to calm every nerve and to give me peace and inspiration when I needed it. Your strength and love are always with me.

My Rock, Christinne, you showed me faith and unconditional love. You gave me a home, a place to run so the world could stand still.

Maria, thank you for believing in me more than I could believe in myself. You showed me how to live without fear. I fell in love with you almost a decade ago, and know without a doubt that our love will last forever. Thank you for the hours of listening, the countless tears and the endless love you gave. I couldn't have made it through all of that without you.

Nancy, we will grow old together, of this I'm sure. But along the way, we're going to blaze a trail. I love you dearly. Thank you for your loving support and beautiful friendship.

To my beautiful Joyce, thank you for lending me your ear, your shoulder, and your love. We shared many a trip to the MAC counter and a lovely Menajouistaxi in NYC. Thank you for telling me "that's not as good as it gets."

DC, thank you for putting my writing into the world and for taking a chance on me. You are a great inspiration to many.

Bob Jordan, I still have that message on my phone. You believed in my writing from the first day you read it. Thank you for supporting me.

Grayson, for approaching me on the rocks and for teaching me about big dreams.

Richard, my number one fan, thank you for believing in me, and for loving your sweet Lady Gia.

Brent, the male version of me, you and Richie never stopped believing in me.

Abby, absofuckinglutely, we were meant to be friends. We put the GO in Chicago. One hundred percent, that's what we are forever, always. And I would go to any McDonald's with you any place, any time. I love you.

Jonny, no fear – that is you – that's what you taught me. God bless you, you're a beautiful person.

Ron, that look on your face that says "Really?" reminds me where I belong, and where I don't. Thank you for loving your sweet friend Gia. You are amazing.

Dad, my sweet Pops in Heaven, may your spirit follow me forever, and forever be in peace.

To my brother, for always loving me, for being a source of strength, and for the great man you are to so many.

Superman, not only are you a great friend, but someone I love and admire. I have seen you at the top of your game, but also when you are just you, vulnerable and real. I think you are a beautiful person. Your friendship and advice have been invaluable.

Joseph, my true love and inspiration…even when you take my lipstick to use as a marker, I love you always and forever.

Mom, I am me because you are you. Thank you for being such a wonderful inspiration, a source of strength, and for kicking my ass. You don't tolerate weakness, and I admire you for your strength.

Stella, Thank you for taking the most amazing photographs and creating a cover that is so beautiful. You are funny and crazy and I'm so glad I met you.

Ashley, you were always there, so I didn't have to be alone. I wish you all the happiness in the world.

Carol, the cover of this book is the greatest gift. Because of your masterful creation with Stella, I have something beautiful to share with the world. Thank you for believing in this project, for being patient with me, and for all of your hard work.

Alicia, thank you for believing in this story and helping me edit it for the world to read. It means so much to me that we have gone through this amazing journey together. Get your laptop out because we have many more to come!

Evie, the whole point of the Chocolate was to meet you. Your belief and support have been invaluable. I love you.

Nicole, you had me at "In transit." I love you, thank you for your support.

To everyone who has been a part of this magnificent adventure. Thank you for loving me, for pushing me, for believing in me. I pray for the opportunity to be a blessing to you.

God, it is because of You my words will touch others. Thank You for Your goodness and mercy.

About Gia

This is a story of honesty. It comes from the heart and is a most candid acknowledgement of life after divorce, of life after change, after the decision to be free from judgment, limitations, and limiting beliefs.

It's not a journey, it's an adventure. And it is for anyone, man or woman, trying to start over, after anything that requires you to dust yourself off and pick your chin up. This is where you can find the honesty to know that sometimes you have to honor yourself, and your courage for making difficult decisions. Sometimes you have to celebrate yourself even when no one else does. Sometimes you have to get a little dirty and make mistakes, but acknowledge that those mistakes are all part of the plan. And sometimes you just have to say "bring it" and jump in to things that you never thought you could or would have. I promise you, you are not alone, and this story will give you strength, hope, and a helluva good laugh.

For 15 years I was married until one day I wasn't. Things change. Dreams change. People change.

I was born and raised on the South Side of Chicago, then moved away to the Southeast for six years. In that time frame, my marriage endured over ten career changes, nine relocations, two miscarriages, and three failed rounds of IVF. Or maybe it didn't. I didn't realize that after spending fifteen years of my life in a business suit that I wasn't dreaming anymore. I worked with some of the greatest leaders in Corporate America, and they inspired me to find my passion, my juice, so I did.

This book is about a woman who found it, the one thing that life is all about. The one thing that must live and breathe in everything we do…LOVE.

I am a single mother living in Chicago with my beautiful son Joseph. He is the most soulful nine-year-old I've ever seen. His eyes dance with possibility, and his heart dreams such big dreams they make me laugh with joy. I am inspired by him, I think he is great, and I am proud to be his mother.

I am alive, and I live. I am a dreamer and I dream. Laugh with me and learn with me.

You have to get a little crazy in life to really get after it. You have to take chances and get dirty. You have to find your sexy. Everybody's got it. Love yourself. Believe in your beauty and show it to the world.

It's cool. We all make mistakes. Don't ever forget that. We all second guess ourselves and doubt if we even know what the hell we're doing. But don't sweat it. There's a plan at work here.

Names and details in this story have been changed to protect those I love and those that are a part of this amazing journey.